AF580607

Rise Above

Rise Above

A Memoir

Matthew Schnipper

Random House
New York

Random House
An imprint and division of Penguin Random House LLC
1745 Broadway, New York, NY 10019
randomhousebooks.com
penguinrandomhouse.com

Hardcover ISBN 978-0-593-73069-0
Ebook ISBN 978-0-593-73070-6

Printed in the United States of America

1st Printing

First Edition

BOOK TEAM: Production editor: Robert Siek • Managing editor: Rebecca Berlant • Production manager: Kevin Garcia • Copy editor: Hilary Roberts • Proofreaders: Janet Renard, Muriel Jorgensen, and Tess Rossi

Book design by Elizabeth A. D. Eno

The authorized representative in the EU for product safety and compliance is Penguin Random House Ireland, Morrison Chambers, 32 Nassau Street, Dublin D02 YH68, Ireland.
https://eu-contact.penguin.ie

For Allegra, Renzo, and Coco

I need to live. I need it now.

—Black Flag, “No More”

Rise Above

When my son Renzo was three months old, I decided it was time to introduce him to the death metal band Morbid Angel. I sat him down on the bed and, on my phone, pulled up "Immortal Rites," the first track off their legendary 1989 debut album, *Altars of Madness,* and hit Play.

I propped him up in the crook of a breastfeeding pillow, as he wasn't yet able to sit up on his own. He was wearing a blue-and-purple tie-dyed onesie with short sleeves. His plump little body contained only curved lines; his arms and legs were still downy. His dark hair was becoming shaggy. He was about 40 percent head at that point, and it lolled around on his neck while the music played.

I was a latecomer to Morbid Angel. I'd heard some death metal when I was a teenager, but I preferred hardcore punk, metal's looser, more feral cousin. Metal, with all its showy guitar solos, felt too put on to me. I wanted authenticity, not performance. If you wanted to be entertained, I figured, go listen to show tunes.

But as an adult, I became more open to indulging a touch of flair. There was an appeal to the music's focus and strength. Played at warp speed with great technical proficiency, death metal was powerful. In its insistence on extremes, it could make you feel euphoric. Hardcore, with its emphasis on cathartic expulsion through yelling, was music that would make you feel not miserable, which is not the same thing as making you feel good.

In the way that you're encouraged to introduce your child to different foods at an early age, I took it upon myself to give Renzo a wide musical palate. I know that, in addition to Morbid Angel, I played him an assortment of metal and hardcore, and so much other music, but those memories, like so many of my memories of his brief life, are gone. I happen to have the Morbid Angel moment on video, so I can revisit it. It took place in May of 2020, nineteen months before he died on Christmas Eve of 2021, after suffering an aneurysm two days earlier. He had something called an AVM, or arteriovenous malformation, in his brain. A malformed tangle of blood vessels, it burst.

Renzo was born with his AVM; his death was inevitable. It was not genetic. There was no way his mother and I could have known, nothing we could have done. One doctor said it was a surprise Renzo lived as long as he did. I don't know if it would have been easier if what happened to him had happened for a terrible reason, rather than for what it did, which is no reason at all.

At the time I played Renzo "Immortal Rights," I had no idea what the lyrics were. As like most death metal songs, the vocals are wholly unintelligible. The singer sounds like a satanic dog, endlessly barking. Listening to the song on headphones at a coffee shop one day, I looked up what was actually being said: "Lords of death, I summon you / Reside within our brains."

As I write this now, it's been almost four years since Renzo died. When I began writing this book, a little more than a year after he died, it was to figure out what happened. Not to Renzo, but to his mother and to me, to our friends, and to our family. His death left mostly questions. Primary among them: How could I keep on living? And why?

It took some time to arrive at answers, if I have at all. I spent a lot of time resentful, thinking about how the government should deliver me a check for a billion dollars to compensate me for my pain and suffering, as though I'd lived through a natural disaster. I'd retire early and set up a hammock in my living room, ride out the next several decades swaying in peace. That didn't happen. I still want it to, to be honest, but it doesn't seem to be coming. So I've had to figure things out on my own. Grief is a difficult thing for people to talk about. No one really knows what to say about death in general, and especially not about the death of a small child. The advice you do get is vague and overarching. Stuff about patience, resilience. Not unwanted wisdom, per se, but loose concepts that are difficult to put into action. I wondered a lot about how to be patient and resilient on the days when it felt like I was melting into the ground.

One way to read this book is simply as a record of how I spent the time after Renzo died trying not to melt. Writing it provided an unconscious catalog of how I changed over time. Early drafts had moments of wild anger, of self-righteousness. I was so angry that I wanted to lash out at someone or something, and I used Google Docs as a place to do that. I'd write down what I thought was an innocuous memory and it would drip with venom. I didn't realize I was doing it at the time, and months later, when I read back these bilious sentences, I was embarrassed by and sad at the way grief had caused me to be cruel. It makes sense, a subconscious pull to fight fire with fire. I don't feel that way anymore. Or maybe sometimes I do, but I now recognize the instinct when it comes and try to accept it, even if I wish it would go away. When I look back at the landscape of the last few years of my life, I see a blackened field. It feels like I crawled through the blaze, and I'm only just on the other side of safety, watching the last embers flicker. It doesn't mean I'm healed, but it does mean I may no longer be in danger.

Before Renzo died, I was not unfamiliar with pain, though of a very different sort than grief. Approaching my teen years, I began to show signs of what would eventually be diagnosed as ulcerative colitis: severe abdominal cramping and a lot of passing blood. To combat the colitis, I was prescribed a steroid, prednisone. For a while, as a small protest against reality, I refused to learn how to swallow pills. My mother would crush each tablet into a powder and sprinkle it over ice cream with chocolate sauce, which I'd eat in the morning before school. It was bitter and made me gag. The prednisone also turned my cheeks into a chubby circle, a side effect known as "moon face."

Though I was never bound for great height, the prednisone stunted my growth, so I was both bleeding from the rectum and stuck at five four. The doctors tried to wean me off the steroid, but each time they lowered my dose, a new side effect took hold. Mysterious aches in my extremities. It felt like I was withdrawing from drugs, which, technically, I was. For a time, as a proposed steroid replacement, I gave myself nightly medicated enemas, but they were unpleasant and not effective. I wanted my body to implode and turn to dust.

As a small boy, I'd loved *Teenage Mutant Ninja Turtles*, the popular cartoon series about four subterranean, anthropomorphic, crime-fighting turtles. As a sick teen, I found myself reminiscing about the turtles because I envied one of their enemies, Krang. Krang was literally a brain with a face; he looked like a pink wad of chewed bubble gum. An evil genius, he survived off his mental agility, eschewed a physical form. If he needed to be mobile, his minions would install him in a transparent compartment nestled in the midsection of a giant robot. This seemed like a preferable existence to my own.

Neither living as a bodiless brain nor continuing on prednisone was a viable option for me, so it was eventually decided I'd have surgery to remove my colon. Or, actually, two surgeries, one where they'd cut the colon out and give me a temporary colostomy bag, and another where after three months where they'd reverse the colostomy, stretch out a portion of my small intestine, and assign it the role of a makeshift large intestine. The recovery period was long. If I was not in bed, I was in the bathroom, my new digestive system working itself out.

This was around the time of my b'nai mitzvah (a joint service with my twin sister, Sara), and because I'd newly become a devoted music fan, many people gave me gift certificates to record stores. The long-defunct chain store Coconuts used gold tokens for its gift cards, and I accumulated a little stash, like a pubescent miser. I used them to purchase the soundtrack for *The Crow,* a gothic antihero movie from 1994. The soundtrack was all dark, moody rock music, befitting of the film. It included Rollins Band, a group new to me, with a cover of the New York City band Suicide's 1977 song "Ghost Rider." The original, which I didn't hear for another decade, is obtusely funky, a nervous hoot. The Rollins Band version is a hostile dirge. I loved it. When the group's eponymous front man, Henry Rollins, yells about a motorcyclist "with his head on fire," I imagined Ichabod Crane on a flaming Harley. At the end of the song, Rollins adds a postscript behind a manic guitar solo. "Keep riding! Never stop riding!" He's screaming at the top of his lungs. His voice starts to shred. "Don't forget to burn! Don't forget to burn. Burn with fire! With fire, fire, fire, fire. With fire!"

As soon as I discovered Henry Rollins, I became obsessed with him. To me, his presence has always been Herculean, gigantic. If you've never heard of Rollins, musician, actor, writer, and buff Los Angeles renaissance man, it may be better to think of him as a fictional character rather than as a real human being. He is the combustible embodiment of Horace Greeley's urge to "go West, young man." He may as well have been pulled from the air by Steinbeck, written with verve as an American colossus at war with circumstance—the circumstance being the basic existential hardships innate to being alive.

Rollins is now in his sixties, but you can imagine him as a younger man, a precursor to Robert Pattinson in *Twilight,* radiating heat, if a touch more feral, magnetic, confused, confusing. Imagine him as a guru, a cult leader, a self-help author pacing the stage, preaching to rapt audiences, expounding on the anguish and humor of pain and all paths to its eradication. He's both George Carlin and Henry David Thoreau, with a touch of John Wick. Imagine him as a lone surfer, cutting through waves as if he were painting brushstrokes against the ocean, beautiful but so alone. Or you can imagine him—this is real, actually—as a guest judge on *RuPaul's Drag Race,* season two, episode six, "Rocker Chick." He has a kind and enthusiastic presence. Perhaps he felt a kinship with the contestants, living monuments to the power of inventing yourself a better life.

In the early eighties, twenty-year-old Rollins joined the band Black Flag as their singer. He helped originate the genre of hardcore punk by thrusting murk into punk's high-pitched freneticism. He had a ferocious presence, both onstage and on record. The music critic Jon Pareles, reviewing the band for *The New York Times* in March of 1983, introduces Rollins as a force: "Henry Rollins, Black Flag's lead singer, showed total control while all about him were losing theirs," he writes. "With every muscle tense, he sang and barked and screeched the group's angry lyrics clearly as he contorted his face and body in almost balletic poses."

Like me, Rollins grew up angry. Angry at his father, his schoolmates, institutions, and expectations. Black Flag gave him an opportunity to funnel his anger into art. That was an equation of relief I envied. "Understand, we're fighting a war we can't win / They hate us, we hate them / We can't win, no way," Rollins bellows in "Police Story." Ostensibly those lyrics are about institutional abuse of power. But if you're twelve or thirteen when you hear that song, as I was, it's about your parents, teachers, kids at school who don't get you. Young and sick, the stakes of everything in my life felt so high that it was a relief to hear that tension echoed back to me. While my physical pain was immutable, listening to Black Flag's music made me feel like its attendant emotional pain could be drowned out.

I used more of my b'nai mitzvah money to buy Rollins's book *Get in the Van,* which is composed of his diaries and memories from his touring days in the eighties with Black Flag. The book is a touchstone for young punks and, in many ways, a harsher document than any of Rollins's music. Despite touring relentlessly and thus spending almost all of his time in cramped spaces with his bandmates, Rollins constantly feels like he is in it on his own. Writing of this searing loneliness, he is clearly in anguish, detailing self-harm and other destructive behaviors. He writes in clipped sentences that reflect his impatience with the wider world. Nobody gets him. I don't know if Rollins's outsider status was a self-fulfilling prophecy or not, but I immediately identified with it.

Escapism, resentment, depression. These were the themes I fed on. It's easy to understand why, too young to understand the faultlessness of fate, I resented others when it was my own body that was the source of so much pain. Others' lack of self-awareness about the privilege of normalcy confounded me. That primal desolation Rollins felt, that I was so moved by, is so clearly there in *Get in the Van.* It's bleak.

> 10/17/84 6:12 P.M. Storrs CT: I think I was born on Mars. I don't fit in with people in the real world. . . . I don't know how long I'd last out

> there in their world. I never remember them until I'm right in the middle of them and that's when I start to freak out. We speak a different language. We say things that make them hate us. For us it's nothing. We hate their fucked up world and they hate ours. . . . My trail will never end. It's lonely because I'm the only one on it. I'm in a band with musicians. I'm not one. Don't know how to play an instrument. Don't want to know. I don't see why all these people like me. I really don't. I wouldn't like me.

There's a video of Black Flag performing that basically sums up why Rollins was so appealing to me growing up. It's from the summer of 1982 at a show at an Elks lodge in Philadelphia, and Rollins is wearing dark pants with a belt but no shirt. His hair is midlength, like he's overdue for a cut he can't afford or make time for. He looks scuzzy. He looks lean and muscly, too, with what I think is a six-pack. But it's an old videotape, and it's not totally clear. He could also just be underfed and sinewy. He bends at the waist a lot, like Gumby.

At this point, Rollins had been in the band only about a year, but he embodied even the songs he didn't write. He is the star; Black Flag is his backing band. "Depression's got a hold of me / Depression, I gotta break free!" Rollins snarls. When they perform that song, "Depression," on record, it's about two minutes long. Live, they stretch it out more than twice as long. It's a bilious, punishing performance.

In the video, one guy in the audience, near the front of the stage, keeps pawing at Rollins. It feels not unfair to say that Rollins appears to be baiting the audience with all his splayed writhing at the lip of the stage. Does he want to be attacked, hoping for a masochist release? Or is some kind of proto–*Fight Club* thing brewing, toxic masculinity with a built-in soundtrack? Whatever he's looking for, be it the freedom to make an empty provocation from on high, for a puppylike tug-of-war, or for a more violent confrontation, is unclear. Rollins doesn't strike first, but when finally hit by the man in the audience, he strikes back. Rollins pummels him: *pow, pow, pow.* He has a big wingspan and comes down on him hard. The guy shrinks back into the maw, never to be heard from again.

To be clear, I don't advocate violence. Even if I did, I'm too small to inflict much damage. But Rollins's whole thing was to me—mad, frail, and afraid—very appealing. On another song, "Nothing Left Inside," he literally yells, "Lonely, lonely, lonely, lonely, lonely boy." Does it get more on the nose than that?

My mother was a nurse at a cancer hospital, later an executive at an HMO. My father was a lawyer, first a union lawyer, then later working in the entertainment industry. Both were extremely supportive of my interests, but they did not share them. Success was about work, the traditional kind, a utilization of skill plus duty. Passion didn't come into it. I looked to the future and saw only what I didn't want. The suburbs, a desk job, a tethered existence. Rollins's life, laid bare in *Get in the Van,* was a vision of success I couldn't have conjured on my own. If pain was a foregone conclusion, I didn't want to also have to cede my nascent interests to the dull mechanics of capitalism. Rollins, an artist, was an avatar of hope, a best-case scenario for the worst case of everything. The last regular job he'd held was at an ice cream shop. He quit to join Black Flag. No looking back. He was a tough guy whose power came from his mind but who had no problem executing with his body. He was hurting, but he was also performing in Sweden. I wanted to go to Sweden.

Rollins told me you have the power to transform your pain into something you control, and thus you have the power to transform your life. He showed me the power of passion, that the love of music and art could be enough to sustain. He showed me more complex lessons, about the wide spectrum of masculinity, about the possibility that the body could be a vector of power, not a burden to be borne. His work ethic showed me that if I was stuck in my bedroom, or anywhere else, because I was in pain, some of the fault for that was mine. He showed me that there was always a way out if I ever needed it. I could always break free.

Twenty-five years after I first encountered Henry Rollins, I named my son after him. Renzo Rollins Schnipper. Picturing my child experiencing any version of what I had experienced made me ache for him before he was even born. I hoped Renzo's middle name might protect him, act as armor. I wanted him to know he'd always have an escape. I wanted him to always believe in himself. To know that he bore the name of a superhero so that he could become one himself. If he was going to be a sensitive boy like me, at least he could also be one like Henry, handsome and loud, willing and able to beat the shit out of anyone who crossed him.

But my fear that Renzo would be born into pain was unfounded. Renzo was not me. He was a sweet, good-looking, serious boy. Until he died, his life was good. He was happy. I was immensely proud of him, loved him more than I thought could be possible. He was the sun, the moon, the stars, the reason for the universe's existence. His simple being obliterated all doubt about pleasure and purpose. There were no more questions; there was only Renzo.

Renzo was born in February of 2020, a split second before the pandemic began. Those first few weeks, in late March and early April, when it was unclear how bad Covid would become, I began posting his photos on Instagram with faux inspirational captions. A picture of him asleep in his bassinet: "He just did nine months in quarantine, you can do two weeks." It seems quaint and naïve in hindsight, but I was so in love with this little boy, a pure miracle, who made it feel like I could survive the then unknowable, that I wanted to share the feeling.

Before Renzo could move around on his own, he spent a lot of time in this thing called a DockATot, a cushioned contraption that looked like a miniature lifeboat made out of pillows. We'd park him in that and put him next to us on the couch while he napped. One day, we had him in the DockATot, dressed in a Black Flag onesie, white with the band's iconic four-bars logo. A friend of mine had given it to him as a gift, to commemorate his namesake. Renzo had fallen asleep with his hand up in the air and his fingers curled into a ball. It looked like he was raising a fist in protest. I took a photo and posted it to Instagram. "RISE ABOVE," I wrote across the photo in capital letters. It's the name of a Black Flag song, one of their most beloved. "Rise above," it goes. "We're gonna rise above, we're gonna rise above!"

Many Black Flag songs are about either the dehumanizing effects of oppression or savoring the violence of fighting back against it. "Rise Above" is different. It's about strength without force. That ineffable quality, resilience. It's a brief moment of hope from Rollins in a career filled with gloom. In between the band chanting "rise above," there is a moving philosophical couplet. "We are born with a chance," Rollins says. "I am gonna have my chance." He sure did. Renzo barely had his. I couldn't change that. Could I still have mine?

When Renzo died, I didn't really think so. I feel differently now, but for a long time, it felt like I was living in a fugue state. Grief made me frustrated with myself and disappointed in others. As I flailed around, hoping to heal, how could I simultaneously be expected to participate in the day-to-day mechanics of life? But everyone is. Most people will not have to live through the sudden death of their child, but most will experience some kind of adversity. Everyone experiences pain. The lessons I learned about struggle and survival are universal. I imagined this book would be a guide. I wanted to write it to help other people. Of course, I ended up helping myself.

There are a lot of things you can say to someone suffering. I'd recommend, though, not telling someone that you can't imagine what they're going through. Because the pain I felt is imaginable, as is yours. If you take the time to imagine it.

I met Allegra, my wife and Renzo's mother, in September of 2015, a decade after I graduated from college. For most of that decade, I was an editor at a magazine, obsessed with my job. My self-esteem was largely tied to my success or failure at work. For a time, it was mostly the former, until it became overwhelmingly the latter. After turning thirty, I started to feel like my life might be better off if it was not defined by my career.

I'd gone through school imagining I'd be a writer of some sort. I wrote short stories throughout college, mostly half-baked scenarios about people missing limbs or teeth. Terrified to leave school behind, I applied for several graduate programs and was rejected by all of them.

With no other prospects, I moved back to my parents' house in Connecticut while I looked for work in New York. In the fall of 2005, six months after graduating, I finally got a job as a salesman for a world music record label. I moved into a basement apartment in Brooklyn and occasionally traveled across the mid-Atlantic to various gift stores and coffee shops hawking CDs of chilled-out Latin grooves. After a few years of that, I got hired at a music magazine, a job I loved and that I allowed to become my whole life, which was useful because outside of working hours I mostly hated myself.

I was no longer physically sick, but the shadow of pain from my teenage years loomed. I had friends but wanted to be in a romantic relationship, though I was generally clueless about what that meant and reluctant to be vulnerable enough to find out. Eventually, on the cusp of thirty, I did fall into a relationship with a woman I met at a flea market. She was often mean to me. She didn't intend to be, but she wasn't a happy person. I felt like cruelty was what I deserved. It was not a good situation, but it gave us both what we needed, which was, for me, to tend to her and to never have to think about myself and deal with all of my problems. I stayed with her because she was beautiful and she liked me. Or liked that I did stuff for her. Whatever the deal was, I wasn't spending too much time hating myself because I was too busy.

One Saturday afternoon, I went to see the Terrence Malick movie *The Tree of Life* alone. The film starts with the birth of the dinosaurs and quickly works its way up to the 1950s, where the actors Jessica Chastain and Brad Pitt are raising a family. It's ambitious and odd, and for some reason

I left the theater inspired to take better care of myself. I would learn to cook, I decided.

I began to make my way through a basic cookbook. I had a minor triumph with scallops. My girlfriend really liked brussels sprouts, so one morning I bought a stalk at the farmers market. I found a simple recipe where you slice the sprouts into half globes and sauté them with salt and pepper. As I cooked, I could see my girlfriend sitting on the couch. She was playing Tetris on her phone. Proudly, I told her how I was preparing the sprouts. She frowned. "That's boring."

That was it. Make your own brussels sprouts. I told her we were breaking up. The next day she called me and asked for another chance. Somewhere between a devout people pleaser and a huge pushover, I was struggling to maintain a position that prioritized my needs over hers. We were on the phone for an hour. I gathered up what few crumbs of self-esteem I had and stuck to my guns.

Why had this been so difficult? What was wrong with me? The gulf between the confidence I felt at work and the lack of it I felt anywhere else was beginning to grow. I started to feel like something was really wrong. So I began to look for a therapist. I wanted someone close to my office who took my insurance. I found an older Jewish practitioner doctor with fuzzy white hair with an office on Eleventh Street. I could take the R train there on my lunch breaks.

After some months seeing him and running through all the ways I felt bad, I asked him if it was possible I had some kind of depression. Maybe I needed to be medicated. He shrugged and said he didn't care much for labels, but, if I wanted, I could talk to a psychiatrist. He recommended another guy with a Jewish-sounding last name and an office in Midtown Manhattan. I made an appointment.

I told the new doctor my entire life story, truncated to twenty minutes. Illness had made my body my enemy. Receding into my mind had helped for a while but was now making things worse. The psychiatrist had a very thin face and he nodded slowly as he listened, like a broken bobblehead. When I finished my narrative, he said it indeed sounded like I had dysthymia, a persistent but mild type of depression. He prescribed me Lexapro, which worked immediately. It's hard to describe having confidence for the first time in your life at age thirty. It didn't provide untold highs but something closer to living at sea level.

It was helpful in finding the courage to look for a new job, as even though I loved the music magazine, it paid poorly. When the editor at a popular tech website offered me a role, I took it. I didn't know anything about technology, but I assumed I could figure it out.

That turned out to not be the case. Knowing a lot about technology is in fact a crucial aspect of working at a technology publication. Lexapro really was no match for the doldrums of tech journalism. The office had a series of tiny rooms for private conversations, glorified phone booths that were probably not firesafe. One day I pretended like I was going in there to work quietly and instead lay down on the floor, balling up a sweatshirt like a pillow, and slept.

A few months after I'd started, the guy who hired me left and the guy who replaced him fired me. The afternoon I was fired, a guy from upper management came to Brooklyn with a cardboard box containing everything from my desk. We met at a restaurant near my apartment and sat, largely silently, over a beer. At some point he got up to leave. I had been nursing my drink and still had half a glass left. I asked him to stay until I finished it so, I said, I could feel like a person. Which he did. After that, I never saw him again.

Later that day, I emailed my friends asking them for help:

> Sending this to my circle of friends in NYC who I am very blessed to know. As some of you know, I was fired today. This is unfortunate for a pretty good number of reasons but not least among them that I have a bunch of weird problems and a lot of infinite time alone is really, really bad for me. . . . I just don't want to go crazy/feel crazy and that's the default option that I am gonna try to push against but I know basically I'll need help to make that not happen. This is embarrassing but whatever. If you have had a burning desire to come over and listen to a bunch of Elliott Smith while I pace, now is your chance. FML? Maybe not?

I cringe reading that email back now. The tone is so glib, so try-hard. Like it would be impossible to be earnest. And while it's good that I was able to ask for help, I didn't realize I could have helped myself. I mostly regret, though, the letter's invocation of Elliott Smith, as though I'd taken the lord's name in vain. As a teenager, I was obsessed with Smith, a folky musician, whose acoustic dirges spoke directly to my melancholy soul. I don't remember writing this email, but I am sure I meant to name-drop him to slyly show that I knew how mopey I sounded, as though self-awareness might negate the mopiness. I wish I could have embraced it.

I first heard Smith on a midnineties compilation issued by his record label, where his solemnity commingled with the breezy rage of music by dozens of punk bands. I had purchased the album for a further avenue into punk and was surprised to instead become enamored with Smith and his song "Big Decision." It's a song about quitting heroin, which I absolutely did not understand at the time. "It's a big decision," he sings. "You can't kick when you're down." I thought it was about not kicking someone when they're down.

After hearing "Big Decision," I bought Smith's first few albums and committed them to memory. He had such a sweet voice, but he made such dark music. He sang about doomed romance, about malt liquor and cocaine. There was a bluntness to his lyrics, a dour realism that made him more Bukowski than Dylan. I was still mostly listening to hardcore and punk and was surprised to find that quiet music could be as emotionally heavy as loud music. I'd thought that what I liked about hardcore music was the anger, the protest. That was part of it, yes, but not everything. It was the intensity, the commitment. Anger was one way to be intense, but it turned out it was not the only way.

In the years I was sick, I listened to Smith's first two albums so much I cannot hear them now without thinking of the forest-green carpet in my childhood bedroom. I'd put on his CD, sit on the floor, and play my old Nintendo. I associate his debut album, *Roman Candle,* with *Castlevania III,* a game that I played endlessly while trying to push through the pain. "All you aspired to do was endure," Smith sings on the album's second to last song, "Last Call." I identified with the sentiment even though I realized it was not a good thing.

Not long after I discovered his music, Smith became

semifamous, performing at the Oscars after his music was featured in Matt Damon and Ben Affleck's breakout film, *Good Will Hunting*. After that moment, Smith largely moved on from the stripped-down sound of his earlier albums in favor of a more baroque style of pop. I was disillusioned by this shift, which felt like an abandoning of his raw principles. This was the type of sanctimonious outrage of my young self I now both scoff at and envy. I still listened to his older albums from time to time but stopped following his career closely. And then, in 2003, Smith died by suicide. He stabbed himself in the heart. His death, so unimaginably horrific, prompted conspiracy theories of murder. Easier to believe that than that someone could be in so much pain they'd do something so gruesome both to draw attention to the volume of their suffering and to end it.

Smith's death brought a surge of interest in his music and gave him a status as a singing martyr to addiction and depression. I bristled at this. His music had been so serious and personal. Seeing him commodified with corny tribute albums and documentaries felt gross. He'd have preferred to be forgotten rather than canonized.

Except I had absolutely no way to know that was true. My presumptuousness about his wish to remain an underground hero served only myself in perpetuating a belief that my understanding of his music was that much deeper than everyone else's. I felt like he'd helped me through real pain, and his new fans only liked his music because they saw it in a movie. This feeling of a proprietary relationship to an artist and their music is one I've tried to erode, but nonetheless it remains.

What was I signaling to my friends in that email, saying

that I was going to be listening to Elliott Smith all the time? That I was depressed and that they should worry, but not too much? Unless they wanted to. I'd be fine. Probably. *FML? Maybe not.*

Some friends did reach out, offering to help. I aggressively applied for jobs, shamelessly asking anyone for any connection I could use to my professional advantage. I had a couple of job offers within a few months. I don't know if it's a testament to my perseverance or my stupidity that I ended up as an editor again, but this time at a men's fashion magazine, in a similar situation as at the tech website, one of authority on a subject of which I had little knowledge. Insofar as I had a point of view on clothes, I advocated for the loose rules of personal style, a tack men's dressing took a few years later. You could say I was ahead of my time, or you could say I didn't know what I was talking about. It was not much longer before I was fired from that job, too.

This time, though, I didn't feel like it was entirely my fault. I couldn't be *so* bad at work that I deserved to be fired twice in a row. Right? Extenuating circumstances, bad luck, etc. I pledged to be nice to myself. I was eager to return to a job in music, where I felt safe, and landed at the music publication *Pitchfork* in the fall of 2015.

I knew through social media that, three months earlier, the daughter of one of my future colleagues, Jayson, had died. Greta was killed in an accident on the Upper West Side. A building long in disrepair had a piece of its façade crack off and fall. It hit both her and her grandmother, who was watching her. Her grandmother was injured badly but survived. Greta, who had just turned two, did not.

Jayson and I didn't really talk about Greta's death in the office. He just wanted to work. All day, he would sit on the couch and hammer away at his laptop. No one has ever typed louder than this man. It was impressive, in a way, his ability to reach the decibel level of an airplane doing a task most people accomplish in near silence. Once I stepped onto the subway and heard someone pounding on their keyboard at an extreme volume. I couldn't believe I had found someone who typed louder than Jayson. Then I looked down the train car and it was him.

Sometimes, though, Jayson would start to cry and walk outside. I spent a lot of time talking to our boss about how to help Jayson but not much time talking about it to Jayson himself, which I regret. When Jayson took a week off to go to a grief retreat, I didn't think too much about what he was going through; I had to figure out how we'd cover for him.

I was thirty-three when I started at *Pitchfork*. It was a good job. I wanted to enjoy it. I didn't want to be depressed anymore. I wanted to get married and have a family. I signed up for Raya, a dating app geared toward creative people. It had no geographic restrictions, with the implication that the kind of person who goes on Raya lives a global lifestyle. It was kind of stupid, but fun. The entire cast of *Saturday Night Live* seemed to have profiles, as did Courtney Love. I matched with both her and Allegra, but I messaged Allegra first.

I asked her out, but she said she was busy for the next week. It was late September, so I asked her if she played for the Mets, who were having an uncharacteristically good season and were on their way to a World Series appearance. A

Yankees fan, she responded with the emoji of a monkey covering its eyes. It was the lead-up to fashion week, she explained. She worked for a fashion brand and was busy setting up its runway show. We scheduled a date to go out a couple of weeks later. I looked around for something to do with her, and it turned out a rapper I liked was performing at Madison Square Garden that night. "Would you want to go to a concert?" I asked. "Sure," she said.

I was given a pair of tickets for the concert by the rapper's record label, a perk of the job, and I had to pick them up at the will-call window. "I should be on the Def Jam guest list," I said to the person behind the glass. If asked how we first met, Allegra likes to recount her inner monologue at that moment. She describes herself being intrigued, if baffled. *What is this guy doing on the Def Jam guest list?* As we got to our seats, I ran into two former co-workers. It had been a few years since we'd seen each other, and they started shouting at me. "Schnipper!" *Why are these young men greeting him like this? What's up with this funky little dude?*

In terms of origin stories, though, the story I really like to tell happened about a year later. We were at a Mexican restaurant in the West Village, not far from where Allegra lived at the time. Before moving downtown, Allegra had grown up on the Upper East Side, a preppy enclave. She went to the school on which they based *Gossip Girl*. The signposts of her life were pointing her toward a more staid, predictable existence, which she resisted. She'd largely been single before we started dating, happily so. A woman of great focus, she was not interested in having a boyfriend who might discount her ambition, a partner who might get in her way.

Seated at a long table across the restaurant were about a dozen men and women, anonymously and interchangeably dressed in the drab worker garb of gray vests and pantsuits. Allegra gestured at them with a mix of compassion and pity. "That could have been me," she said.

I like that story because it makes me feel good about myself. As though I'd rescued her and brought her into the pleasingly weird world she'd always imagined was out there but hadn't yet discovered on her own. It's self-aggrandizing—it's not like Allegra wouldn't have been fine without me—but it's also a little true. But what had she given up?

Would she have chosen that other life, dull but predictable, if she knew then what would happen to us—to her?

Six months into dating, Allegra and I took a vacation to Sedona, Arizona, to see the rock formations and go hiking. It was a wondrous place, impossibly orange, and I loved it. But after a few days of strenuous hikes, on the side of a mesa, I found myself at the end of my bodily abilities and I freaked out. Were we lost? It was getting hot. Could I do several more miles of this? "I'm Jewish!" I blurted out. I meant it as shorthand for my neuroticism. I can't say she was head over heels at that exact moment, but she didn't shame me. She understood I was anxious. She also laughed at me. And then she reassured me we were not far from the parking lot.

When we first began dating, to explain herself to me, Allegra told me a story about when she was a girl. When she was turning twelve, her parents told her that if she wanted to have a birthday party, she would have to plan it herself. Uncowed, she set up a sit-down lunch at Planet Hollywood for twenty kids. Her mother found out when the restaurant called to ask her for credit card verification. Allegra could handle herself. She didn't need me; she wanted me.

I remember on maybe our fifth or sixth date, in the liminal period between casual and serious, watching her come up the stairs to my apartment, a third-floor walk-up that she'd eventually move into with me. That's the day I started to commit her to memory. She was wearing a Barbour jacket with a corduroy collar, a preppy staple. Her oval face, her chestnut-brown hair, so much hair, then long and straight and pooling on her shoulders. She'd eventually cut it to a bob and let it grow wild, a world of waves and curls. She worried it looked too triangular. She wasn't totally wrong, but I loved it. Allegra responds well to plans, organization, logic. That she'd let her hair go untamed signaled a secret spark of freedom and chaos inside her.

I felt like I understood her better than anyone in the world had ever understood anyone. I felt like I understood her better than she understood herself. This may have been presumptuous, but it elated me, calmed me. I had not known that self-discovery could include another person.

Early on in our relationship, Allegra told me she didn't care about marriage, but she knew she wanted to be a mother. She was surprised when I agreed with her about parenthood but not about marriage. I wanted to do things in order; I did not want a child out of wedlock. An ancient point of view to a modern woman. But she was okay with it. I bought her a ring as we neared our second anniversary. I couldn't figure out how to propose. Allegra doesn't like grand gestures. So I winged it. We'd moved in together and ordered a new couch from a company in California, and after months of waiting, it finally arrived. A tremendous day.

Sitting on the couch together, doing the crossword, I told her I had something for her. "Is it a fidget spinner?" she asked. She was excited. This was the summer fidget spinners were popular. I'd already bought her two. "It's not," I said.

A year later, Allegra and I were married at the University Club, a 150-year-old social club housed in a hulking Beaux Arts building in Midtown Manhattan, where her father is a member. Women were allowed to join only starting in 1987, and there's a pool in the basement where men still swim nude. Aside from the pool, there is a formal dress code, jackets required. You have to borrow a loaner if you don't bring your own. We were married in a small room off to the left of the main wing where, before they were allowed as members, women were permitted to wait for men to finish doing whatever they were doing. Allegra wore a custom dress, white with red flowers. She looked so beautiful.

We'd hired a DJ for the party, but we needed to figure out what to play during the ceremony and immediately after. The choices were relatively obvious; we'd walk down the aisle to an orchestral piece by the composer John Adams and then, after the vows, we agreed we'd of course play house music.

There is a scene in the movie *Beginners* about house

music that perfectly captures its universal appeal. The basic premise of the film is that Christopher Plummer's character, Hal, late in life, comes out as gay. His relationship with his adult son Oliver, played by Ewan McGregor, has been strengthened by Hal's new discoveries, but there's an undertone of resentment about how the repressive side effects of his being closeted affected how he parented Oliver as a child.

Hal does his best to navigate his relationship with Oliver, but he's also trying to make up for lost time and is often too besotted with his new life to tamp down his enthusiasm. After going to a dance club one night, he calls Oliver to gush.

"They had some wonderfully loud music!" Hal says, then imitates the bass and drum sounds with his mouth. "*Untz untz untz untz*. What kind of music is that?"

The movie flashes to a scene of Hal on the dance floor, spotlit and blissed-out, shirt unbuttoned past his clavicle, swaying from side to side like a cattail in the wind.

"Probably house music," answers Oliver. He's in bed.

"House music!" repeats Hal. "House music. Okay!" He grabs a pen and writes it down. A discovery now with a name.

My own discovery of house did not include a sexual awakening, but it did make me realize music could provide more than an escape from pain, that it could also be a window into pleasure. I understand how Hal felt in the club. He felt free. A dance floor is a much less scary place than a mosh pit.

Allegra and I decided, specifically, to play music by the house musician legend Mr. Fingers. His music emphasizes breeziness, weightlessness, and fantasy. His songs have names like "Waterfall," "Waves Against the Shore," "Beyond the Clouds," "Dolphin Dream." We played a few songs from his album *Cerebral Hemispheres,* a reference to the two spheres of the brain. (It is impossible for me to see any reference to the brain and not think of Renzo and his death, even though our wedding was in 2018, two years before his birth. But still.)

I loved our wedding. All our family and friends were there. Our friend Daniel officiated. He towered over Allegra and me, this tall, slim, and handsome man offering his blessings from up high. He pronounced us married, and we pressed Play on Mr. Fingers and glided around the room.

I wanted to be married for a year before we tried to have a baby. I wanted to make sure we could survive one of each of the 365 days as a couple. That was important to me, enduring the comings and goings of the seasons.

And we endured them fine, with a trip to Italy for Allegra's friend's wedding, one to Spain for our honeymoon. Not much of a stress test. Allegra bought a notepad in the shape of a heart and handwrote me little missives when she left the house in the morning. The worst thing that happened was we had to move when our top-floor walk-up apartment kept flooding and the landlord dragged his feet about fixing the leak. The new place was a few blocks away from our old place. We got movers, but I walked over some of our most precious stuff.

Allegra got pregnant easily, and her pregnancy was relatively smooth. She had morning sickness, but she got so used to it that she'd get up from breakfast at the diner, head to the bathroom, puke, and come back and eat her omelet. On her birthday, five months pregnant, Allegra built an IKEA crib for another pregnant friend and her husband, who felt overwhelmed by its mechanics. Then we went out for ice cream.

Our only major source of conflict was a name for the baby. I wanted something classic, anonymous. Something that would not define him before he defined himself. I have a mixed relationship with my own name. Matt. It's a curt word. Something you step on. Solomon, a strong contender for me, was an early veto. Allegra wanted something Italian. We were at a stalemate. Arthur was a possible compromise, but it was a lowest common denominator, a name about which neither of us was passionate. We decided to wait until the baby was born and let him decide for us.

Renzo was due in late January, but his due date came and went. In those last two weeks before his arrival it seemed like he might not actually arrive at all, that the pregnancy was a delusion. I made plans for dinner a week after the due date, sure that they wouldn't need to be broken. I was right. Eventually, nearly two weeks past her due date, Allegra's water broke in the late evening, around eleven. We headed to the hospital in a cab in the dark. The driver said nothing during the ride but wished us well as we got out, which was nice.

The nurses set us up in a big room and told us to hunker down until the morning. Allegra opted out of the epidural for a bit, until she opted in. We slept on and off, watched some of *Black Panther* on her iPad.

It was February 4, three days before my mother's birthday. She'd had the same birthday as her own mother-in-law, a glitch of fate that created years of difficult, shared celebrations. We imagined that if she had the same birthday as her grandson that wouldn't be so bad, but we weren't trying to push it. My grandmother had died about a decade before; the seventh had been my mother's alone for some time. The nurses assured us there was no way the baby would still not be born three days from now; no need to worry. That was the last lighthearted conversation we had with any medical professionals for a while.

After a day of labor, it was clear that, whenever it happened, Renzo was not going to come out on his own. "We recommend you have a C-section," the attending doctor told Allegra. "Recommend?" I asked. "What are the other options?" None. Die.

Soon Allegra was on an operating table with a curtain separating her upper and lower halves. I was seated on a stool behind her head. She was vomiting and shivering. That's normal, the anesthesiologist told me. It didn't seem like it. I was trying not to panic.

And then the doctors lifted Renzo from her abdomen and raised him in the air to show me. He looked pale, a chalky purple. The pediatricians in the corner looked him over. I started crying. He was fine, they said, and they brought him to me. Allegra was in and out of consciousness. I held him up to her face. "Our baby," I said.

As I held him, my firstborn child, I waited to be flooded with serotonin or whatever chemical love is made of, but it didn't come. My attention was on Allegra. She was not in good shape. A call went out over the PA for additional bags of blood. People were hurrying. I asked the doctor nearest to me for reassurance that she would be fine, which I did not get. So my need got bigger and my fear deeper. "Is she going to die?" I asked the room. "Will she be able to have another child?" I was holding Renzo, born into a commotion. I was in my right mind enough to take a photo of him on my phone and text it to his grandparents. "He's here." It was the morning of the sixth. My mother would have her birthday to herself.

Shortly thereafter I was invited to hand Renzo back to the nurses and leave the room while they sewed Allegra up. Soon they brought her and Renzo to meet me in a recovery room. Allegra was dazed but okay. Renzo began to nurse. I put on his diaper, my first. I did it backward. We watched eagerly as the nurses swaddled him. I asked them to teach me and they encouraged me to try. I wrapped him to the best of my ability, the loose knots unbinding. I was scared to go as tightly as needed. He was so small. Impossibly small. Delicate, like a cloud. Here he was. Our baby.

When she was pregnant, Allegra had been imagining she'd give birth to a little boy who looked like me, her stocky, bald Jewish husband. Instead, he looked like her: pursed lips, round nose, relaxed eyes. Italian. Renzo, she wanted to call him, a name we'd discussed but not seriously. After what she'd gone through, I felt like she could name him anything she wanted.

We spent five days in the hospital, Allegra recovering, me trying to figure out how to help, how to fit in. Renzo was a sweet baby with no issues. When we brought him home, our landlord, Gordon, who lived downstairs, greeted us. "That baby's got a lot of hair!" he said, and he did, not surprising given his mother's wellspring of locks. Gordon gave us a candle.

It's impossible for me to separate those first few months of parenthood with the ensuing pandemic. The feelings I had about each swirl and collide in my memory. It was stressful. I know having a baby is not rocket science and we are not idiots, but landing at home after the discombobulation of Allegra's emergency surgery was exhausting and scary; simultaneously learning how to be a father was daunting. It would be a month after Renzo's birth before lockdown began in earnest, but the news was looming. The beginning of the Covid quarantine was a period filled with confusion and fear. Though we weren't going outside much anyway with a newborn, there was a genuine fear that if you so much as saw another person on the street, you'd die. At one point I was convinced I had Covid. I checked my temperature secretly in the bathroom every hour, waiting for confirmation that I was infected. It never came. Renzo was not an afterthought, but he was not the only part of the equation, as we had imagined he would be.

He slept in a bassinet beside our bed. "Slept." Some of those first nights I sat on the floor holding him, letting him suck on my finger, hoping both he and Allegra would sleep. Before he was born, I'd taken a class about parenting for fathers. The teacher had encouraged us to be awake with our partners whenever they were feeding the baby in the middle of the night. "What do you do while she is breastfeeding?" I asked. You make coffee, the instructor said. Allegra and I don't drink coffee. So I looked at eBay on my phone while she fed him. It was not a chatty time.

I remember Renzo asleep on my shoulder, sitting on our couch near the window, soaking in the late-winter sun. He was an amenable little baby, often dressed in a onesie with golden moons, wrapped in a blanket illustrated with various dogs in primary colors. We called him Renzo Potato, because he was like a little sack of potatoes, easily transportable.

Allegra's recovery from the C-section was complicated by an infection that took months to heal. She could not sit up well. We ordered a bedside rail so she could hoist herself to her feet. We rolled up two large canvas blankets into tubes, like portable armrests, which we moved from room to room, bed to couch, and back so she could feed Renzo or, if he was napping, to help her try to sit up straight to watch something on TV. We watched *Gilmore Girls,* a show about motherhood under unexpected circumstances.

Every night at seven everyone on our block would open their windows to clap and hoot to celebrate the healthcare professionals dealing with Covid. At the time, quarantined and hopeless, this daily ritual was the only bit of community we had. We lived not far from a hospital, and EMTs would sometimes idle their ambulances in the no parking zone across the street from our apartment while waiting for a call. We'd see them eating takeout in the front seat. It was nice that we could cheer for them directly. I wondered if they parked there on purpose. All the neighbors would wave at one another. We'd hold Renzo up to the widow, a little nugget of hope for the future. Little did we know. Maybe we were idiots.

"We." It seems obvious if essential to note here that the

parallel structure of a couple's "we" naturally shifts with the introduction of a child. Renzo was dependent upon his mother for nourishment and comfort of a kind I could not provide. I have read that it takes some time before babies realize that they are their own being, distinct from their mother. That is accurate to our experience with Renzo. Selfishly, I wanted him to be indistinct from me, too. But it doesn't work that way. Once he was born, our lives were about him. Some of the necessary tasks I could do: change diapers, rock him to sleep, read him books, etc. But I could not breastfeed him, provide him sustenance, even if I wanted to. Allegra, on the other hand, had grown him, she'd suffered through his birth and its agonizing aftermath.

Had he lived longer, Renzo's time as a baby would have been a fraction of his life. As it was, it was basically all of it. We were both his parents, but not in the same way. I was his father, she was his mother. By definition, his death could not have affected Allegra and me equally. In practical terms, that means this story can really only be our story, both Allegra's and mine, up to a point. This is my version. There is, as of now unwritten, Allegra's story, which I am being careful not to tell on her behalf. But some borrowing is necessary. I've done my best not to do so presumptuously, but presumption by definition is built into speaking for someone not yourself. I am sorry to have selfishly roped her into this venture, but for me to make it through, I saw no other way forward.

One of the first times I remember making Renzo laugh was when I started spinning two white gym socks in my hands like airplane propellers. He was sitting in his little rocking chair, smiling up at me, astonished.

I lived for attention from him. But I dutifully returned to work in May, after my three months of paternity leave from *Pitchfork* ended. It was the pandemic, so "returned" means I logged on to Zoom meetings from the bedroom all day so Allegra and Renzo could have use of the living room and kitchen. In place of a desk, I piled a bunch of hardcover books on the windowsill and balanced my laptop on top of the stack while I sat at the edge of the bed talking into the computer screen. It killed my back. That lasted for three weeks until I was laid off. The company was making cuts due to the slowdown in ad revenue related to the pandemic. I'd seen it coming, which offered no satisfaction.

The only silver lining of the whole thing was that I could care for Renzo when Allegra returned to her job. We decided that, because we had the privilege to do so, it would be easier to leave the city and live at my parents' house on Cape Cod. We decamped from New York in June.

It's silent at night on the Cape. We'd gotten used to the sirens in the city. My parents were not there for the beginning of our stay, both parties opting to quarantine before cohabitating, and so the house was relatively still. Allegra brought her computer to the deck and took her meetings from a glass picnic table.

Most days, around noon, I'd take Renzo on a walk in his stroller, either down to the beach or very near it. The neighborhood was a maze of roads, and over time we went down each of them. No one was ever around, and so we sauntered down the middle of the street. It felt a touch postapocalyptic. There was one road by the water that I loved. We would always go down it. It was marshy, with birds and long grass. As we walked, I'd talk to Renzo, tell him about the scenery, about the painted mailboxes, the windowless jeeps and old cars in the driveways. One house had a huge garden and I'd point out what they were growing, the mint and the basil. There were wild rabbits everywhere. "Bun-buns," I called them. I'd count them for him on each walk. It was so hot every day, blue sky with no clouds. His stroller had a nice canopy to keep him from getting burned. It blocked his peripheral vision, so I'd spin him around so he could see everything. After his second nap, we'd sit in the front yard on a blanket, periodically moving across the lawn to chase the sun as the day wound its way down.

Renzo lived a bountiful life out there in Massachusetts. A whole house to himself! He established a close relationship with a green plastic flour scoop. He'd hold it proudly in one hand like a scepter. One day he crawled around the living room clutching an envelope, so I called him "the mailman" for a little while. He was obsessed with the latch on a small locked wooden box on a bookshelf. When my parents arrived, I asked my father what was in there. "The dog's ashes," he said. I moved it to a higher shelf.

I'd always played Renzo music, but he started to really respond to it at around six months old. Harnessed in his high chair, captive to lunch, he bopped and clapped along to "Ma Foom Bey," an eighties house song with a chanted chorus made up of nonsense words. He loved disco, too, once sitting on my shoulders and clapping along maniacally to "In the Bush" by Musique, a song it later occurred to me was not exactly appropriate for a baby.

His light brown hair started growing shaggy and his face went from circular to narrow. He took off his socks constantly. I noticed one day, toward the end of a long walk on a wooded trail, that he had one bare foot. We retraced our steps for what felt like miles with no sign of the missing sock before I gave up and turned around. I swear to god he looked me in the eye, smiled devilishly, and telepathically told me how much of a sucker I was.

On those walks I'd sometimes call friends and catch up. I

often spoke to Daniel, our wedding officiant, who was quarantining in Portland, Oregon, with his mother, his sister, her husband, and their children. A musician, Daniel was in Brooklyn College's Sonic Arts grad program, which had moved online. He'd gotten divorced not long before, and though he was in a relationship, it was long distance. He had no job, and out in Portland he had a lot of time to think.

Daniel and I met at the end of 2001, when we were both freshmen in college in Washington, DC. Two weeks after I arrived was September 11, 2001. I watched the Pentagon burn from the roof of my dorm. The next two years brought anthrax scares and the DC sniper. It was a strange and paranoid time, but my life was rapidly expanding, as was my music taste. About a decade after I discovered hardcore punk as a vehicle to channel all my rage, I discovered there was much more music out there, and more emotions, too. In college, I found house music, disco, techno, jazz, and blues. I found some friends, too.

I lived near a store that sold used video games, cassette tapes, CDs, and records, and nearly every day I'd walk up Eighteenth Street's hill to where it plateaued at Columbia Road and step into the now-defunct CD Game Exchange. Many of the records went for ten cents apiece, and I would buy them by the armful. I became friendly enough with the staff that they let me sneak behind the counter to get first dibs on new arrivals. I wanted to hear everything; I bought so many records that I think I got close.

Daniel, too, had been mesmerized by Henry Rollins as a boy. Reading *Get in the Van,* he said, radicalized him in five minutes. Now in college, he was having a similar trajectory of discovery outside of hardcore punk music. But where I was an observer of musical life, Daniel was a participant, an adept and innovative guitar player. I wanted to be around him all the time, for whatever he had to rub off on me. I met him because I was a big fan of his band, a five-piece called Black Eyes. He introduced himself to me at one of the band's shows at a café in northern Virginia, as I had become a familiar face in the crowd. His fellow band members were older than him, in their midtwenties. We were still teenagers.

When he performed, Daniel let himself flail around, often inadvertently hurting himself or other members of the band. He was seemingly unable to control his limby body, like a baby giraffe taking its first steps over and over. But he had no hang-ups about this clumsiness; if anything, it was a source of pride. I watched with awe as, eating dinner at a Mexican restaurant before a Black Eyes concert, he spilled a tub of queso on himself and then went on to perform with dried cheese caking his shirt. I remember, at another show, watching him pretty badly smack one of the band's two drummers in the head with his guitar's headstock. Everyone kept playing.

I joined the band on tour as a roadie the summer after my freshman year of college. Daniel and I crammed ourselves in the backseat of a rickety old passenger van, beside the rattling drums and amps, making jokes about everything as we drove across the eastern half of the United States. We stopped at record stores in every city, culminating in a much-anticipated visit to Pittsburgh's Jerry's Records, the shop then commonly known as one of the largest used record stores in the world. Some of the band members had been urging me to get further interested in jazz, and at Jerry's, in a room full of records dedicated to the genre, I picked up an album by the saxophonist Ornette Coleman, *Free Jazz*. The cover featured an image of Jackson Pollock's painting *White Light*, a representation of the explosive quality of the sound. On the album, Coleman's saxophone alternately soars and screeches, and the wildness of the music, frankly, shocked me. Partially that was because of its age. *Free Jazz* was from 1961, rage music from decades before hardcore's inception. You know what Henry Rollins was doing in 1961? Being born.

The friendship Daniel and I formed facilitated more and more artistic awakenings, more new doors opening, Daniel always delighted by possibility and delighted to share. New bands, music, films, books, people. Discovery for me had been a solitary experience. Sharing music with Daniel changed that. Our friendship made my world bigger because it made me happier. Catharsis was good; joy was better.

During my Covid walks, two decades into our friendship, calling Daniel to discuss the day's comings and goings was a way to recharge. Though I loved spending all day with Renzo, I felt tired and alone. I missed seeing friends, having co-workers. After losing my two previous jobs, *Pitchfork* had been the thing I was going to get right. Getting laid off because of reduced advertising revenue due to a global pandemic was not my fault. I wasn't fired because I'd done something wrong. If I had, at least I could learn from it. This was bad luck. There was no lesson to learn from bad luck.

As Renzo slept in the stroller, lulled by the sea air, Daniel and I would talk about the frustrations and fears of unemployed pandemic life. I'd applied for job after job, writing cover letters for roles I wasn't qualified for or didn't even want. I took an online audio production class, hoping to bolster my skills for any roles in the then-booming podcasting industry. I sucked at it. Talking to Daniel moved what felt like rote failure out of the realm of the miserable and into the one of the narrative. The facts were the facts, but at least they were mine to recite as I pleased.

Daniel was working on a new album for one of his solo projects, and we talked often of his progress. One day he brought up one of his old songs, "Boi." In the beginning of the song, he said, was a long introductory section made up of ugly noise. The source of the sound was a recording he'd made on the city bus, then stretched out using audio software. It sounds like a magnet breaking apart. That goes on for about a minute before the song's rhythm kicks in. The intended effect was to create a primordial soup for the song to crawl its way out of, Daniel said, but, listening back, he realized he'd overshot it. It was too much dissonance. A minute of disorientation was too long to wait for the payoff. A few seconds would have done the trick.

Time passed and things eventually started to perk up. In the spring of 2021, I was offered a temporary position at the media company Vice, filling in for an editor who would be going on maternity leave. It would last four months. I accepted, relieved to have a real role to play.

Suddenly, we needed to scramble for childcare. We returned to New York, where we signed Renzo up for daycare, but that wouldn't start for a month. So we arranged for my friend Rachel to watch Renzo. She, too, had been laid off during the pandemic, and she was living at her parents' house near the beach on the Cape, doing yoga on the porch, playing with the dogs, baking incredible breads and pies. Since she didn't have anything else going on, I asked if she wanted to watch Renzo for a month. Why not? she said. So we returned to the Cape.

Best Friend Rachel, we called her. Renzo lit up when she arrived each morning. She took one of my all-time-favorite photos of him. She didn't show it to me at the time, because he was in direct sunlight and she was afraid we'd be mad she'd let him get exposed. But she showed me later, after he died. She caught him as he lay on the wood floor, peaceful and content, glowing in a brilliant ray like a cat on a sill.

After a month with Rachel, we returned to New York. I cried the first day we dropped Renzo off at daycare. I felt like I was abandoning him, like I'd chosen a job, money, myself over him. I cried because I didn't want this to be reality. He cried, too, which didn't help. But we all got over it quickly. About fourteen months old when he began, he was a wobbly walker. After a week with the other kids, he was steady on his feet.

Things settled. Vaccines were on the way. You could touch other people, as long as you washed your hands afterward. Renzo's life, which had belonged only to his parents, began to belong to the world. This was a welcome shift, if a difficult one. The pandemic bred closeness, the feeling I'd always desperately desired but struggled to cultivate. But as much as I missed having him to myself, it was a thrill to watch him enjoy the company of others, embrace the bigness of life. I remember how Renzo strolled around our neighborhood one day, holding the hand of my friend Jacob, a man with an enormous beard, the two of them a ridiculous pair, Renzo in his car pajamas and tie-dyed Crocs ("dye-dye," he would say), Jacob like Santa Claus in his early forties. The three of us ate pizza like we were a trio of buddies hanging out. After we finished, I changed Renzo's diaper on a wooden bench. We were on the other side of our neighborhood at the time, venturing far afield for grandma-style slices. The pizza place is now just a block from our new apartment. I sit on that bench from time to time.

I remember how Renzo liked to loudly declare that he was running. He would take off his diaper in his bedroom and run naked down the narrow hallway to the bathroom for his bath. "Running!" I remember the way he stomped along the sidewalk in front of the neighborhood elementary school, which had been painted with large polka dots. He called out the color of each as he stepped on it. I remember how he pronounced "yellow" as "yay-ow." It was, like him, very sweet.

I remember singing to him every night while he was in his crib, sometimes a reworking of the song "Daylight Matters" by the singer Cate Le Bon. The original chorus goes, "Love you, I love you, I love you, but you're not here." A sad song, but I guess I wasn't listening too hard, because I didn't realize it before I refashioned the lyrics. "I love you, I love you, I love, Mr. Renzo, yes, I love you," I'd sing, a lullaby stripped to its barest essentials.

I remember in the summer before he died, we started to sing "Take Me Out to the Ball Game" to him every night.

We abbreviated the title to “Ball Game,” and when I said “Ball Game,” he knew that meant it was time to go to sleep. He’d protest. “No ‘Ball Game,’ ” he’d say, unless he was very tired, in which case he’d acquiesce, lie down, and listen to me sing.

I remember he slept with his butt up in the air sometimes. He wanted to bring his Crocs into his crib before bed, and we’d let him hold them but not sleep with them. When he got old enough for a blanket and a pillow, he wasn’t interested.

I remember he hated all jackets except his green jacket. We accidentally taught him to say “so handsome” because we so often said he was so handsome. He was so, so handsome.

I remember how he loved Christmas decorations. Walking around the neighborhood in the winter, the weeks before he died, leaning forward in his stroller as far as the straps would allow, hoping to reach garlands hanging on fences and in trees. I remember he laughed at “silly walking,” when people would waggle forward with bent knees and splayed feet. I asked everyone to do it so he’d be happy. I remember when a grasshopper landed on his jacket sleeve on the playground one evening and he watched it under the streetlights, mesmerized. I remember taking him for a four-hour-long outing, an epic journey where he walked up stairs by himself for the first time. I remember he was wearing his orange-striped pajama bottoms and his white-and-red Nikes. I remember I’d never felt more proud of anything in my life.

I remember having smoothie night every Monday when Renzo and I were alone while Allegra was at pottery class. I’d get out the blender and he would stand on a small stool at the counter and help me dump in dates, frozen blueberries, oats, cinnamon, a banana, ice. When the blender was grinding those up, he'd shake his head from side to side to imitate its frenetic movements. A day after he died, when everyone was ordering lunch for delivery, I got a smoothie. I don't know why. Maybe I thought it would honor Renzo. It was a bad idea. When it arrived, I doubled over in pain.

Renzo's life was not unique. He was a little boy who did little-boy things. The types of memories we cling to are plain, the ones you'd otherwise forget. His death changed our future, but I did not imagine it would change our past.

When my father's father died in 2013, my father asked me to write the obituary and I agreed. I was able to paint my grandfather in broad brushstrokes. A product of the Great Depression, he was a penny-pincher, but he loved the thrill of buying a new car. He was tall with a reedy face. He was quiet. He liked reading the sports pages. All of these things were characteristics I'd learned from the thirty-plus years we shared, along with input from my father about their relationship. There was plenty of material to draw from.

When I speak about Renzo now, I fall into a similarly sweeping narrative. It's how you speak of the dead, with praise and generality. He was a serious boy, I say, though I quickly follow up to clarify that it's not that he was a curmudgeon but that he was considered in his approach to play, preternaturally dignified. And then I freeze. What else can I say? How do you remember the life of someone with whom you were never able to have a conversation? How do you prove you loved him? That he loved you? That your relationship, however brief, was so all-encompassing that his loss blasted a hole in you the size of the universe? A memory of twirling socks feels like thin evidence. But it's what I have.

~

There is a painting by Marsden Hartley that I love, that I first saw at the Metropolitan Museum of Art on a high school trip to New York City. Marsden was from Maine, but he lived for a time, in the 1910s, in Berlin. He became friends, perhaps lovers, with a German military officer, Karl von Freyburg, who later died in World War I at twenty-four years old. Hartley's painting, *Portrait of a German Officer,* contains images of flags, pendants, and the Iron Cross medal for bravery that von Freyburg was posthumously awarded. Despite being called a "portrait," it does not contain von Freyburg's face or any other corporeal depiction of him. No hands, arms, legs, knees, feet. No nothing. But it is his essence, a portrait of his being and of his having been. Seeing this as a teenage boy, standing before this enormous vertical canvas, confounded but excited me. How could there be a person without a person?

I think of that painting now, painted to memorialize the death of a young man, and I think of Renzo, who was still in the mode of becoming but whose brief life contained so many of his own flags and pendants. He could be remembered as parts, with no need for a sum. There need be no grand statement for an indelible impression to still be made. One hundred years later, here stands German officer Karl von Freyburg on the wall of the Met, outliving us all.

The day Renzo had his aneurysm, or, as I sometimes call it, plainly and avoidantly, "the day it happened," was not the day he died. Technically, that came two days later, on Christmas Eve, in the hospital. But he was gone the day it happened. Or, rather, the night. We actually had a really nice day before that. I remember some of it.

He was supposed to have been at daycare, but earlier that week there had been a Covid scare and they closed. Allegra and I were in the final steps of buying our first apartment and, to settle some paperwork, had planned to go to a nearby pharmacy where a public notary worked, as well as to Citibank. We walked over with Renzo. The bank had a small parking lot with a long, sloping ramp, and while Allegra was inside, Renzo showed me how he could walk down it backward, which he did very slowly. Allegra got a cashier's check totaling the sum of our life savings, and we moved on to the pharmacy. The pharmacy was in the middle of a busy block, so while we waited, Renzo and I snaked around to a side street that was mostly empty. Dead leaves were piled between the curb and the wheels of the parallel-parked cars. Walking up and down the street, holding my hand, he looked at his reflection in the car windows and finally stopped in front of a shiny car door, which stretched and shrank his body like a fun-house mirror. But he knew it was him. I took a photo of him preening on my phone that I've never been able to look at. I think the car was black.

I put him to bed that night. I don't actually remember doing it, but I know, shortly after he died, that I made a point to remember that I had. I assume I sang "Ball Game." I assume he ate dinner. I assume he sat with Allegra on the blue chair, because that is what he liked to do. I know that, for a little while, he was asleep.

And then he cried out. This wasn't unusual. He had been waking up once a night most nights. We thought it was teething. Usually Allegra would go to him, as she did that night. He loved her so much. He had been going through a bit of a Mom phase around the time he died. "Dad's not bad," I would say sometimes if he was touchy with me, a modest mantra.

Allegra got out of bed and I went back to sleep. Only for a moment, but I remember I had begun to dream when she woke me up. "He's being weird," she said. He appeared to be asleep, but he'd gone limp.

You do not imagine that your child will die. Or maybe you do, but always in the abstract. At the parenting class I took before Renzo was born, the teacher talked about trusting your gut to know when something was wrong. One guy said that his own father had saved his life as an infant by giving him CPR after he suspected he was not breathing. Such a close call. But "close" is as far as you ever believe things will go.

"This might be ridiculous," I said to the 911 operator, "but our son won't wake up." She did not think it was ridiculous. Soon an assortment of firefighters and EMTs arrived at our front door. In the ambulance, unconscious, Renzo had a seizure. I watched his body shake. But the EMT was nonplussed. "It's a febrile seizure," he said. "Pretty common stuff." That would prove to be incorrect, though it seemed promising at the moment. The EMT took a video of Renzo so we could show the doctors. I asked him to text it to me, but he was sheepish, so I used my phone to take a video of the video on his phone. He made it seem like this would be crucial evidence, but it was not needed.

At a nearby Brooklyn hospital the doctors did a scan, which confirmed there was a large amount of blood in his brain. They did not have a pediatric neurologist available, so they called around to find a hospital that did. It was the middle of the night. I lay down on the tile floor and asked for some water. I drank that quickly and then went to the bathroom several times. I called my parents and texted my therapist. I did not know what to do because there was nothing to do.

Allegra realized she did not have her phone. I called Gordon, our landlord, who we knew hardly slept, and he retrieved it from our apartment and walked it over. When I picked it up from him in the waiting room, I remember not wanting to be rude and cut the conversation short. Soon after, my mother-in-law, Marianne, arrived. Ambulance transportation was arranged for Renzo to be transferred to Weill Cornell Medical Center, a place I will never go again. Only one parent was allowed to accompany him in the ambulance because of Covid rules, so Allegra went with him while Marianne and I took a Lyft, which is a leisurely way to arrive at your own son's death.

At first, the doctors felt confident that Renzo would survive. They didn't say it clearly, though. "The chances are low that he won't make it," one said early on. We misheard. "So you're saying he's not going to survive?" "No," she clarified, "he likely won't not."

The doctors were nice. The nurses were nice. Everyone was nice. One doctor had Crocs with bluish lightning on them. I thought they were a reference to the cover of Metallica's album *Ride the Lightning* and asked him about them. He was a neurologist; he said they were a reference to the electricity in the brain.

We met the surgeon who would be operating on Renzo, a trim, gray-haired, handsome man. We did not know it then, but he was the same doctor who operated on Jayson and Stacy's daughter Greta.

After a day at the hospital spent mostly awake, I crashed. My parents and sister arrived in New York, and they went to our apartment to bring Allegra and me clean clothes. I asked them to bring me my CPAP machine, too. I was using it diligently then. I set it up beside the orange couch next to Renzo's bed, careful to not mix my tubes with his. It uses distilled water, and I asked the nurse if they had any. She said she'd get some. "We don't want you to go apneic," she said, as though that were something that mattered.

There's an old brainteaser asking you to identify, from a jail cell of newly arrested men, the one who is guilty of his crime. Most of the men are wide-eyed and nervous, but one is sleeping soundly. He's the guilty one, because he knows he's been caught. There is no longer anything to fear, because consequences have arrived. I'm embarrassed to admit I slept ten or eleven hours that night. At that point we were still being reassured that Renzo might survive, but I knew. Seeing him in the hospital bed, sallow and still, it was impossible to believe the same wonderful boy we knew was present in that body. If that were the case, he would have woken up. He was gone. A parent knows.

The doctors were avoiding being straight with us about Renzo's condition. I get it. No one wants to be the person who says a child is going to die. If he did come back, I asked one of them, would he ever be himself again? They hedged but said that no, after that much bleeding in the brain, he likely would not. That was a terrible outcome I hadn't considered; life or death on the binary was as far as I'd gotten. Something in between was a new possibility. But spending time worrying about it didn't seem necessary, so I did not.

My friend Dean came to the hospital to take a walk with me. I needed the company and the fresh air. Dean was resolute in his belief that Renzo would survive. I appreciated his faith—his unqualified urge to always look on the bright side was why I was friends with him in the first place—but it felt misplaced, not like reassurance but like denial. I'd seen what I'd seen. You don't come back from that.

When we woke up on the second morning, the redheaded doctor who had been with Renzo overnight told us it was time to gather family. I appreciated her honesty. I sat with her in a break room and showed her a video of Renzo dancing to OutKast in his Christmas pajamas. I wanted her to know he was a real person. He did a little spin on my phone screen. She took out her phone and showed me a video of her son, about Renzo's age, dancing naked. It felt at that moment that we would be connected forever. That I would see that little boy grow up, that we'd be bonded by the inverse power of tragedy. But I never saw her again. I don't even remember her name.

I texted and called people, asked them to text and call people. One friend called me to say that when she got my text, she was in the car with her husband and daughter having a disagreement about if he did or did not pack her a sandwich. The news, she said, had made them stop fighting and remember what was really important. It was the first time my pain was a lesson to others.

I needed to call my therapist. I found a quiet spot by some service elevators and again lay down on the floor. The only other place to lie down was on a stretcher. Two hospital employees exited the elevators and saw me on the ground. "Are you okay?" they asked me. "My son is dying," I said. They left me alone.

I'd been seeing my therapist for a few years at this point. She was caring and thoughtful, but she was a practitioner with a job to do. She rarely gave anything close to advice, so when she spoke up with a directive, I listened.

"I'm going to kill myself," I told her.

"You can't," she told me. "Allegra won't survive that."

There's been some discussion between her and me in the time since then that what she actually said was "Allegra *shouldn't have to* survive that." Not *won't*. A small difference, but enough that what I heard was that my voluntary destruction would cause her involuntary destruction. It was what I needed to hear. I couldn't cause her more pain.

A nondenominational, nonbinary minister came to our room. They asked us to give thanks for each part of Renzo's body. His arms. His legs. His eyes. Thank you, Renzo, for your belly button.

Eventually the other doctors came around to the same conclusion as the redheaded doctor. The numbers were not going in the right direction. It was Christmas Eve now. Did we want to consider organ donation? Yes. A man from the organization said he'd rush over. He lived nearby, and despite the holiday, he'd be there soon. He arrived wearing a tie, which I thought was respectful.

It was time. We said goodbye. Allegra and I held hands and walked to her parents' apartment, not far from the hospital. It was cool out, but not unpleasantly so. We did not want to go back to our apartment and in fact never did again. There was no longer anything there for us.

We slept on the foldout couch in Allegra's parents' living room. When we woke up it was Christmas. There were questions to consider. What do you do after the worst thing you can imagine actually occurs? Literally, what do you do, where do you drag your burdensome body and freshly maimed mind? In the immediate shadow of such an incomprehensible event, where do you spend your waking hours? How do you live when your life is over? I had no interest in mulling over the answers. We spent the day screaming, crying, and watching season two of *Emily in Paris*. It had just premiered. We let the episodes wash over us.

On the show, both frictionless and enveloping, naïve,

American Emily, having moved to Paris for work, charms all the stuck-up French people with her Midwestern pluck and colorful outfits. It's so stupid, as was the need to do anything at that exact moment. Days prior, we couldn't find time to shower. Everything was Renzo. Now all we had were empty hours ahead of us, spread out before us like a wasteland. A punishing abundance of time. On the screen, the playwright Jeremy O. Harris showed up in a campy cameo. "Oh, look," we unconsciously said aloud, a knee-jerk recognition, "there's Jeremy O. Harris." That we'd noticed was unfortunate confirmation that our brains still worked.

Our friend Alex came over to keep us company. My parents were there, Allegra's too, as was Puccini, their panda-like papillon, who himself would be dead within a year. He liked to sit on the back of the couch, lording it over everyone. If I was lucky, he'd put his paw on my head. Renzo's photo was everywhere. It didn't yet hurt to look at it.

Another thing my therapist said to me as I was lying on the hospital floor was that I was going to have to ask for what I wanted. She said this like it was the most obvious thing in the world. Maybe it was. People, eager to help in the face of a tragedy, would want to help but would not know what to do. I was supposed to tell them. I spent much of the next year figuring out what I wanted. The conclusion I reached was that what I wanted was for my son to not have died. How could I possibly want anything else?

People began to mobilize, circling us, not unhawklike. They did all want to help, which was kind, but it was true that they had no clue what to do. I could picture them, lined up at the ready, bouncing on their heels, eager for their assignments. It was nice to hear from a wide network of people, but I did not know what someone I hadn't spoken to in years was going to do for me now, in my most intimate time of need. I found that it was easy, at least, to ask for help with basic things. Sure, order me a sandwich. No, I don't care what kind.

The purchase of our new apartment had gone through without us while we were in the hospital. We were the brand-new owners of the home that we'd bought to raise Renzo in. It was painted mustard yellow. We'd arranged to have it painted white, which was going to take a week. So our friends rented us an Airbnb. It was a kind gesture. Dean organized it. He found a nice place in our neighborhood, but in a different corner of it from where we'd lived, which made sense for the alternate version of our lives on which we were about to embark. The pictures on the Airbnb website showed the place had two floors, plenty of space for mourners.

Brian, a close friend from college and my first roommate in New York, said he wanted to come and stay with us for a while, to fly in from Berlin, where he'd settled and had a son, Miles. "You're going to be an uncle," Brian had texted me one day in early 2019. A few months later, I was able to say the same thing to him. I was heartbroken that Miles and Renzo would grow up an ocean apart. They knew each other from FaceTime, at least. To Renzo, Brian was Uncle Brian. To Miles, I was *der Papa von Renzo*. A lovely mouthful.

At first I pushed back on Brian's insistence. What a hassle for him, for his family. But it would be such a comfort to see him, and I relented.

We spent two days at Allegra's parents' apartment. On the morning of the day we moved to the Airbnb, Allegra and

I met my former *Pitchfork* coworker Jayson and his wife, Stacy, for a walk in Prospect Park. What I was looking for, I knew, wasn't resolve or comfort. It was guidance. It had then been five years since their daughter Greta had died. The simple fact that they were still alive proved that our survival was possible. I hoped they'd tell me their secrets. Or at least mercifully smother me in my sleep.

There is an Albert Brooks film about being dead, *Defending Your Life*. In it, Brooks and Meryl Streep, both newly dead, find themselves in a waiting room to heaven. They undergo a trial, and if they're judged to have lived morally enough, they'll proceed to heaven. If not, they'll have their soul dropped into a new body to try again. I've always thought of our walk in the park as something like that trial, a less playful if equally bewildering midpoint between life and death. Jayson and Stacy didn't pass judgment on us, but they did recommend books, support groups, yoga, a visit to the comically literal website Grief.com. We took them up on every piece of advice. They were the experts. From far away, Jayson pointed out a tree they'd planted in Greta's memory. I later looked it up on the list of trees planted in the park. It's a black gum tree near Vanderbilt Playground. There are thousands of trees planted in Prospect Park on people's behalf. Largely in memoriam, but there are some for weddings and birthdays, too. The stuff that happens to everyone.

Everyone will experience grief. Death happens. Usually it's expected. Sudden death is more unusual. Sudden death of a child is rare. I'd always viewed Jayson as a funny, sweet, passionate person. But because of what happened to him, I used to regard him as someone categorically different from me, different from everyone. Someone in his own world who, after what he'd gone through, deserved a wide berth. In the park that day, he and I were no longer different. Here he was, standing before me, showing me who I would become.

The truth is I don't remember too much about that walk. I was still in shock. I do know that, toward the end, as we exited the park and walked back toward the street, my grandmother called me. It was the first time I'd spoken to her since Renzo died. My mother had been concerned the news might actually kill her. She was in her midnineties by then. When she called, I was looking for a bathroom. Did that park welcome hut have one? No. We were about to try the smoothie place by the movie theater. I answered the phone and my grandmother told me about how she had thrown herself on the floor when she heard about Renzo. She'd consulted a therapist. She said she had a dream that Allegra and I would have another child, a baby girl. I was standing on a rock, shifting my weight from leg to leg, trying to distract myself from having to pee.

Allegra and I took a taxi from the park to the Airbnb. In the bedroom was a king-size bed, which I managed to occupy all of. Lying in bed felt comfortable, and I was aware comfort was dangerous. Like I might never get up. I asked Allegra for a few minutes alone. I needed to call a rabbi.

In 2010, I was asked to apply to an invitation-only network of Jews called Reboot. I was interviewed for fitness at a Thai restaurant on Twenty-third Street by one of the organization's leaders, a British guy with a popular soccer podcast, and accepted. Several months later I was on a plane to a resort in Utah where about a hundred Jews from New York, LA, San Francisco, and London, a consortium loosely defined as people working in media, social justice, and the arts, discussed whatever we felt like.

After a day of mingling, it quickly became clear I was out of my element. I was one of those Jews who felt ineffably, quintessentially Jewish but who hadn't done anything religious since I was thirteen. People here were wrestling with god. I went to a panel about being neurotic. There was a semispiritual Shabbat service that involved walking blindfolded down the side of a mountain. I sat it out. As I was taking a quiet moment to myself one afternoon, a bald man with glasses came up to me. "You're my doppelgänger," he said to me. It was Damon Lindelof, co-creator of *Lost*. He was right, we did share a bald-guy-with-a-round-face-and-glasses look, I thought, but was I not better-looking? I asked a woman I met at the conference. She said yes, nominally, but that was likely all I had on him.

Despite my misgivings, in the years since leaving Utah, I've stayed on the Reboot email list, a lively place for discussion of Jewish issues, self-promotion, and people looking for subletters. On the night he died, Christmas Eve, I sent an email to the group. My motivation in writing was a nonbelief in the situation at hand, not so different from the email I'd sent to my friends years earlier when I'd lost my job. I wanted to throw up a flare, to ask for help. More so, I wanted someone else to fix it.

"My son Renzo passed away today," I wrote.

> He suffered an aneurysm caused by a malfunction in his brain that was present at birth we would not have known

about. He was a fantastic child who could speak Spanish (from daycare) and English, he was very funny, sweet, loving. A shockingly warm and happy little boy. His presence brought such a profound change to how I understood the vastness of life. He was 22 months old.

I know a lot of people have gotten comfort from this community in similar times. Those who know me know how devoted to him I am. I am not always so religious but this is a time I would like those who are to think about him and perhaps someone experienced in this maybe could reach out directly. I'm not even sure what I'm looking for to be honest. But I wanted to write here as I thought others might be able to help. If not just think about him. He really liked people and held hands with new people that he liked. A recent photo is attached.

Thanks and love
Matthew

In the photo, Renzo is sitting on the floor of our apartment, dressed in his green sweater with a train on it. He never grew big enough to properly fit into it, but it was a gift from Alex, and so we liked to dress him in it. In each hand, he's holding a rubber ducky. One of them is dressed like Santa, who it did not occur to me is not Jewish. Looking at the photo again now, I'm surprised that Renzo looks a lot more like me than I remembered.

Many people responded (but not Damon Lindelof). It did help. They offered love and prayers, the least they could do, though also the most. One woman whom I'd met at the conference started her note by saying, "We don't know each other." It made me laugh, at least.

The leader of Reboot suggested I contact Rabbi Sharon Brous, whom the organization often worked with. I googled her. She'd recently led a Passover service at the White House. It seemed like I would be in good hands. I wrote to her and she emailed me back quickly, and we scheduled a time to talk a few days later.

On the phone, in bed at the Airbnb, I tried to explain to Rabbi Brous the liminal state I felt like I had entered. The thing that popped into my head was Samuel Beckett: "I can't go on, I'll go on." She laughed and told me to hold on a minute. Then I got a text message from her; it was a photo of the mug she was currently drinking out of, which had "I can't go on, I'll go on" printed on it.

She encouraged me to set up a shivah at the Airbnb. "Sitting Shivah at the Airbnb": It sounded like the title of a magazine article about how the gig economy desecrates ritual. But it could work.

In Judaism, shivah is the seven-day mourning period immediately following a death. The close family of the deceased gather in a home while mourners come and go. There are rules: People should sit on a short stool or a pillow to signify the low mood. Men should not shave and mirrors should be covered, as there is no need for vanity while mourning. The doors should be unlocked so people can enter without disturbing the bereaved. Shivah, Rabbi Brous said, meant we should not leave the house and should do nothing but think of Renzo. In other words, what we were already planning on doing for the foreseeable future.

As we spoke, I looked around for a sheet large enough to cover the mirror in the bedroom. The only one I could find was a fitted sheet. I placed it over the upper side of the frame and it drooped loosely. I remember thinking it looked like a squid, or a piece of modern art. Though it stayed up for the week, unfortunately, soon after my call with the rabbi, I did shave. It wasn't about vanity; I needed to excise the days of hospital stubble. I figured god would not hold it against me.

Rabbi Brous suggested I gather a minyan, traditionally a group of ten Jewish men, and say the kaddish each day as part of the shivah. She said I needn't be too strict on the number or gender.

I was familiar with the kaddish, the mourning prayer, from attending Hebrew school as a boy. The prayer, she explained, isn't even in Hebrew. It's in Aramaic, an ancient language. (People have been mourning for a long time.) The kaddish has an English translation, but comprehension seemed beside the point. She did not attempt to explain its literal meaning. Reciting it in its original language, she seemed to be saying, was like casting a spell. She sent me a link to a transliteration:

> Yitgadal v'yitkadash sh'mei raba b'alma di-v'ra
> chirutei, v'yamlich malchutei b'chayeichon
> uvyomeichon uvchayei d'chol beit yisrael, ba'agala
> uvizman kariv, v'im'ru: "amen."

Sounding this out was a task, but I was glad to be told what to do, to stand naked before death and attempt to heal myself with ancient ritual. To not be so cosmically alone.

A bag of clothes materialized on the floor of the bedroom of the Airbnb. I'd given my sister a list of what I wanted, and she'd fetched it from our apartment. The packing list is still in my phone's notes app, synced across my devices for eternity:

Black running sneakers under my dresser

Two tshirts

White hoodie with apple on it

Marlowe granados book on the shelf

Nyc blue baseball hat on hook behind door

long blue light jacket on hook

One of the T-shirts Sara chose was a Nirvana T-shirt that she didn't realize no longer fit me. I gave it to her. The white hoodie was from Briermere Farms on Long Island, a farm stand with legendary pies that we had gone to with Renzo the previous Memorial Day during a trip with friends. It rained that whole weekend. I bought the sweatshirt as a souvenir. I'd asked Sara to bring me that hoodie because the gray one I'd worn to the hospital I never wanted to see again. I needed the light jacket because I had only my winter coat with me. I'd grabbed it as I left the house in a hurry, heading to the hospital, and it was not actually that cold out for December. I never finished that book, and I don't know who I was kidding thinking I might go for a jog.

It had been three days since Renzo died. My parents had returned home, exhausted. Brian arrived from Germany. I was so relieved to see him, but I felt so guilty for feeling even a tinge of happiness. Within ten minutes of his arrival at the Airbnb, the doorbell rang and he went down the stairs to answer it. I was irritated he'd invited someone over without asking me, and then I realized it was his weed delivery guy.

People wanted to feed us, so we made a list of neighborhood restaurants we liked and suggested favorite dishes that could be ordered for us. Patatas bravas arrived multiple times a day. Deliveries of croissants, bagels, babkas accumulated en masse. When someone dies, people get you carbs. I ate them by the fistful.

People came to visit. Friends, colleagues, random people we hadn't seen in years. Two friends who visited brought their babies. They asked if we were okay with it, and we said yes. In retrospect, I really wasn't.

Though they were babies then, both of these two kids who came to the Airbnb are much older now than Renzo ever got to be. It's difficult to comprehend that these children I know as happy toddlers, who go to soccer, who are potty-trained, who talk to me about their dance class and their sneakers, were once so small, little specks of people compared to the big boy I was raising. How, in the time since he died, has everyone else done so much living?

Allegra sat on the couch wrapped in a synthetically soft blanket that had arrived in what was labeled a "comfort box." Soup, a ladle, a blanket. I cannot remember who sent it. She was working on her bead loom, a small device she'd ordered that allows you to create beaded bracelets with complex, colorful patterns. It's intricate and tedious work that requires great focus. I watched her disappear into it.

I was scared about what would happen to us. Would our marriage be a victim of Renzo's death? If we ever escaped this black hole, would we find that, back on Earth, our love for each other still remained? Jayson had told me a story that both comforted and concerned me. One day, in the hospital with Greta, Stacy had looked at him and asked if he wanted a coffee. He did. So she went to get him one. At that moment, Jayson said, he knew that, despite what had happened, she still had enough room to love him. I envied his self-assurance. As I said before, Allegra and I don't drink coffee.

Stacy recommended we post the news of Renzo's death on social media to get the word out beyond our immediate community. In the past, she said, an obituary would have run in a local paper. Everyone would know. Social media was the closest thing we had to a town square. Not having to alert people individually, she said, would be a small relief.

I was reluctant. The more people knew, the more real it would be.

In the past, when I shared Renzo's photo on my Instagram stories, I used the "close friends" setting, where you limit who can see your story, though I had a very liberal definition of both "close" and "friends." I liked showing him off and did so constantly. I was not shy about how proud of him I was, how happy he made me. Sometimes I worried that maybe I was too aggressive in posting his photos. Then I had the thought that if someone didn't like it, they could unfollow me. This was *my* Instagram, he was *my* son. I could do what I wanted.

So it made sense to tell people on Instagram. It had been a vehicle for celebrating his life and now would be one to grieve his death. On the morning of December 27, I wrote in white text on a black background:

> Hi close friends—many of you know but I wanted to tell people who regularly see his photo here that Renzo died. He had a rare condition we would not have known about and had an aneurysm and could not recover. Because of the pandemic we shared a lot of photos here and you were a part of his great life too. So if you're reading this I just thought you should know.

Not particularly poetic. But what else was there to say? How else could I say it? Was there a "better" way to convey such a thing? Allegra wanted me to include the reason he had died so there was no speculation. It was important to her that people understand we could not have known about his condition, that there was nothing we could have done. It did not occur to me that anyone would think otherwise. It broke my heart for her that this was something she felt she had to consider.

Many people responded. Most admitted they had no idea what to say. I didn't mind that; I didn't really know what to say either. Most people were generic in their condolences, but not everyone. I got a series of text messages from a guy whom I'd known for a long time. They were weird.

> I love you I love you I love you, my whole heart and brain reached out of my body toward your house, I can't imagine the weight and sickness that must be on you now. You have a beautiful genius brain that will know the world in previously unimaginable new ways, but today must be so so so hard. No need to reply ever but you are head-squashingly on my mind and I am ready and willing to help if/however I can.

What I wanted to say was *What the fuck?* What I actually said was "Thank you." He kept going.

> Well if you ever need a nonjudgemental sociopathic sounding board, I know I'm far from inner circle, but always be curious to hear what you're going through. One foot in front of the other, eh?
>
> All I'm saying is I wouldn't make the pitiful face or drown you in sympathetic taglines. You gotta be in some wild ass territory right now, just trying to clumsily send some sincere compassion and love.

Shortly after this exchange I dropped my phone down the stairs and it cracked into pieces.

I've thought about these messages with some regularity in the years since he sent them. I know why I bristled at them; they were odd. Yet the thing I have come to realize is that he wasn't wrong. I *have* seen the world in previously unimaginable new ways. The question was, what would I do with this new view? Yes, things would never be the same, but just as crucially, in most ways, things *wouldn't* change. I'd have to go back to work, pay my taxes, scrub the toilet. I'd have to keep living, just like everyone else. But not at all like everyone else.

On Mondays, Reboot held a Zoom kaddish. They'd started doing it during the pandemic as a weekly space to mourn the dead. There were so many. Rabbi Brous encouraged me to join.

I dialed in from the main bedroom of the Airbnb, the computer perched on a tall desk perpendicular to the large bay windows. The light was nice. Alex joined, standing beside me. We logged on to Zoom and found that many people were online and in the meeting. The moderator went around, asking people to say who they were there to say the kaddish for. A number of people, Reboot members who had received my email, said they were there for Renzo. I was touched but crushed. If strangers on the internet were taking time out of their day to mourn someone they'd never met, it said something about the enormity of that loss. That they might have been coming to support me didn't really cross my mind at the time.

After everyone introduced themselves, we were asked to stand and step back from our computers to recite the kaddish. The intention was that the sound of us all reading broken Aramaic through our computers would produce a choral effect. And it did. It sounded haunted, a butchered Zoom prayer played through laptop speakers. It sounded ancient, like witchcraft.

Like when Renzo and I listened to Morbid Angel's "Immortal Rites" without knowing the words, I still didn't know the meaning of the kaddish at the time we recited it. I looked it up later that day. There are competing English translations, but it appears to largely be a plea to an almighty god to create peace. "Blessed and praised, glorified and exalted, extolled and honored, adored and lauded be the name of the Holy One." Eight adjectives—it feels a bit like laying it on thick. "He who creates peace in His celestial heights, may He create peace for us." It's clear that whoever wrote this knew how much of a difficult spot they were in.

After we logged off, Alex began to cry. He's a tough person and he said he felt embarrassed. He'd tried to be strong, to support us, he said, because how did he have a right to be sad after the loss we'd experienced? But it was his loss, too. To Allegra and me, it felt like Renzo had been ours alone. But Alex knew Renzo. Many people did. We were starting to learn that his life was bigger than the two of us, and so, too, would be his loss.

It was difficult to figure out how to spend our time. Continued distraction seemed like the only viable option. The idea that we might try to reckon with healing someday loomed, but not yet. There was a massive television in the bedroom beside the now-covered mirror, and Brian had brought a list of movies to watch. We tried the Beanie Babies documentary, but after a few minutes of seeing children onscreen we shut it off. We had more success with *Spy,* a very funny and very ridiculous Melissa McCarthy movie we'd seen before. While watching, I was texting with a friend, and I insisted that she see it. I was so serious about this, I sent her four dollars via Venmo so she could rent it. I think I was trying to be an enthusiast, the part of myself I liked best. But it was performative normalcy, which I assume came across as shell-shocked and awkward. My real self had disappeared.

We watched a couple of episodes of *Younger,* which is a TV show about a woman who pretends to be younger than she is to get a job in book publishing. It has several seasons, and I could picture myself binge-watching it, hours of my life given over in these characters. But was that how I wanted to engage with the universe at that point? It was not. Disappearing into a screen held a strong appeal, but I worried it was a step beyond escapism and toward nihilism. I was already spending a lot of time in the bathroom watching TikTok, which is about as close as you can be to not living while still being alive.

I wanted to listen to music. There was a small collection of records at the Airbnb: Crosby, Stills, Nash & Young, Miles Davis's *Kind of Blue,* a compilation of folk music. We played each one and the music sounded fine, but listening to someone else's records felt uncanny, like wearing someone else's shoes. When I thought about what music I wanted to hear, the singer Bill Callahan was the first artist who came to mind, so I asked a friend if she could go to our apartment and bring over my copies of his records. Once she did, I played them on repeat. I was looking for a guide, for someone to tell me what to do. Perhaps it could be him.

Callahan has a voice that's broad and deep, like he's the bard of a bog. His songs are simple, folksy. Oftentimes he sings about the stuff he does to fill time, like staring at a spinning ceiling fan or drinking beer in the woods. In 2005, when he was still recording under the name Smog, Callahan released an album called *A River Ain't Too Much to Love*, which is a title that hints at meaning something without actually meaning much of anything. The album has songs that feel similar, impressionistic vignettes that he uses as microcosmic metaphors about the simultaneous pointlessness and privilege of being alive. There's one about finding an abandoned well and yelling obscenities into it. There's another where, at a bar, a woman tells Callahan he has an ego "the size of Texas." "I'm new here," he says—"here" being Texas—"and I forget: Does that mean big or small?"

There's defiance in there, too, nestled among the jokes and the gestures. One gloomy song, "Say Valley Maker," concludes with a rejoinder to mythical banishments: "Bury me in wood / And I will splinter / Bury me in stone / And I will quake / Bury me in water / And I will geyser / Bury me in fire / And I'm gonna phoenix." An invincibility anthem that, in the depths of early grief, resonated, if intimidated in its totality. Elsewhere in the song is a sweeter description of perseverance that always gets stuck in a crevice in my mind.

It's about horses, a frequent lyrical subject for Callahan. "Oh, I cantered out here, and now I'm galloping back." That type of triumph seemed more poetic, more manageable. A gallop was something I could realistically aspire to.

The Callahan song I like most, and the song I've arguably listened to the most in my life, is *A River Ain't Too Much to Love*'s closing number, "Let Me See the Colts." It's also nominally about horses. "Let me see the colts that will run next year / Show them to a gambling man thinking of the future." I loved this idea, this simple way of looking ahead, of inevitably.

When we held Renzo up to the window at seven when everyone clapped for the nurses, that's what we were doing. "Thinking of the future." I did not realize at the time it was an inherently hopeful act, but I do now. Despite how things turned out, I don't regret it.

I've listened to "Let Me See the Colts" a thousand times and it's always a perfect song. On the stereo at the Airbnb, it was a relief that something still was. At the end of the song, when Callahan does finally see the colts, he asks, "Is there anything as still as sleeping horses?" He repeats himself, seemingly stunned, and then the album ends.

If I wasn't going to kill myself over the grief, if I had to deal with my new life, then I wanted to do it like a character in one of Callahan's songs. I wanted to heal myself from Renzo's death by wading into the dust on a stallion, drinking away my pain, and returning to society with the hurt burned away. I really thought it would be that simple.

Another Callahan album I listened to was called *Sometimes I Wish We Were an Eagle.* I wished we were, too. Soaring around in the sky, beloved, sounded good. Maybe I could bring Allegra and Renzo. The album included a song called "Eid Ma Clack Shaw," where, in a dream, while "working through death's pain," Callahan sings, "all the answers" come to him. Half asleep, he scribbles them on a notepad. In the morning, he wakes to discover he's written down gibberish: "Eid ma clack shaw / Zupoven del ba / Mertepy ven seinur / Cofally ragdah." Callahan recites it like it's gospel. I understood it as much as I understood the kaddish, which is to say both not at all and with every fiber of my being.

Rabbi Brous had offered to host a Zoom service of sorts on the seventh and last day of our shivah.

That morning, Allegra was needlepointing on the couch, an ongoing project for a friend. The canvas said, "Think happy thoughts." Before Renzo died, when she was sad or angry, Allegra was the one who needed to get moving, go outside for a change of scene, while if I was upset, I preferred to be home and ruminate or nap. We'd switched. I could feel the pull in me to socialize, to not slow down, like I was trying to outrun the grief, to drown it in light. I knew Allegra felt differently. It was not that there was a gulf between us—if anything I felt more connected than ever to her, the only other person in the world who understood what I was feeling—but when we were together, that meant there was no reality other than our own, no buffer, no levity, only Renzo, only grief. The pull of the black hole was strong. We would have to depend on people and things external to us to prevent us from sinking. We knew we would have to spend time apart to heal. That this was necessary felt like an additional punishment.

Some people would be joining us in person for the service, and, as I wanted some time to gather myself before they arrived, Brian and I took a morning walk. Allegra stayed home. It was rainy out, but not enough that we brought umbrellas. We took a right out of the house, headed east toward Bed-Stuy. On the corner, we saw the actor Michael Cera. I'd seen him around the neighborhood from time to time, but he was pushing a stroller now. I didn't know Michael Cera had a kid. I googled it. "Is Michael Cera a father?" According to the internet, he was not. I didn't think much of it. Maybe he was babysitting. But months later, while he was doing a promotional interview with the comedian Amy Schumer for their show *Life & Beth,* she accidentally let slip that his wife had had a child. He'd been keeping it a secret. "Is that public knowledge?" she said. "I just outed him. I just outed his baby." Cera's preference for privacy felt completely foreign to me. How could you not want everyone to know?

Brian and I cut up to Bedford Avenue, where we passed a store with a sign in the window advertising records for sale, five LPs for twenty dollars. Did we have time to browse before people started gathering? Who cares? I said. Things weren't going to start without me. We went inside.

The place was split between two rooms, with the front area crammed with records overflowing from stacked milk crates and the back housing an enormous old TV with several grizzled men huddled around it, watching a conspiracy theory–style video about how the Constitution says you technically don't need to have a driver's license to operate a vehicle. The scene felt totally bizarre, which gave me a feeling of relief. My favorite thing to do was to dig through endless piles of records (and other trash) in strange establishments, hunting for treasure.

Despite the plethora of albums, this was not a promising offering. Most of the records were moldy or warped, scratched-up DJ copies of nineties soca and reggae singles. I picked up crate after crate, maneuvering my way around the small room, finding nothing worth buying.

Then a man got up from the television and handed Brian a small pile of records from behind the counter. He flipped through them and quickly passed me two LPs: original pressings of punk records from the early nineties. Both records are rare, selling for several hundred dollars apiece. Among a roomful of thousands of essentially worthless records, it made no sense that they were there, like finding diamonds in a gravel pit. I was thrilled, which I immediately felt guilty about. As we were paying, the proprietor told us he had a storefront a few doors down filled with records he could show us. It had no electricity, but he could daisy-chain a lamp or two. I wanted to go, but we had to head home to mourn.

When we returned to the Airbnb, people had begun to arrive. Some wore dresses or suits, long black coats. Respectful clothing. They chatted quietly. The service would take place on my laptop, which I set up on the kitchen counter, so everyone assembled around it. Rabbi Brous logged on to the Zoom and talked about, I don't know, probably healing. I have no memory of what she said. Everyone later assured us that it was moving. My father and I led a reading of the kaddish, our final recitation of the prayer.

At the end of the ceremony, I gave a small, extemporaneous speech. I held up the records Brian had found. "These are a symbol of the possibility of my continued desire to be a part of the world, to not retreat," I said. "Because if you retreat, you might not find rare records."

Stop and smell the roses, basically. Even encircled by darkness, I would find beauty. So could you. This was what my teenage years had taught me, that the euphoria of discovery could go a long way toward counteracting the dull gravity of pain. Maybe that's what I meant. But that's not what I said. What I said was that I was glad I got a good deal on some pricey collectibles and maybe one day you could, too.

I didn't talk about channeling my grief through art. I didn't say I was excited to actually listen to the music on the records, only to find them. In truth, I didn't even like one of the albums and the other I already owned. What I didn't realize I was saying was that I was glad I got really lucky. That's nice, but luck is not actionable, not sustainable. I might as well have encouraged everyone to keep living because every once in a while they might find three hundred dollars on the sidewalk. But I was trying to give everyone a pep talk, to tell them not to worry too much, to prove to them I was okay when obviously I was not.

It is customary at the end of shivah for the bereaved to leave the house and walk around the block to symbolize a willingness to return to society. The mourners, our community, would walk behind us to symbolize their support. I liked this idea; I like symbolism.

Rabbi Brous had encouraged us to play music that Renzo liked as we logged off Zoom and filed out of the apartment. We chose "Levitating" by Dua Lipa. When we pressed Play, people laughed. But Renzo loved that song. He'd sit on the floor, legs splayed in front of him, and bop up and down while we played it on repeat.

It's a great song, a modern take on disco, which was arguably Renzo's favorite genre. Unlike some of the more ribald classic disco songs we'd listen to together, it's sweet, with only hints of innuendo; Dua Lipa's target audience is a little too young for the explicit stuff. "I believe that you're for me, I feel it in our energy / I see us written in the stars." It's how I feel about Renzo and how I hope he felt about me. It's a love song, but there are many types of love.

Allegra and I walked downstairs and out of the Airbnb onto the street, "Levitating" wafting out the front door. We took a left and then a left again and found ourselves on Atlantic Avenue, a multilane road that runs east–west across Brooklyn, all the way from the East River most of the way to JFK airport. It's a pretty rough street, filled with potholes, which was fitting for our reentry into society.

New Year's Eve showed up, a week since Renzo had died. Brian and I decided to take a walk in the evening. I asked Allegra if she needed anything from outside, a custom in our relationship when one of us leaves the house. The answer is usually no, but that night she did have a request: diet ginger ale. During her pregnancy with Renzo she drank an ungodly amount of diet ginger ale. I got addicted, too. In the pandemic, we had cases of it delivered to the house. It was our evening snack, taken over ice, a mnemonic device to remind us to try to relax.

Over time, we'd identified a hierarchy of diet ginger ale brands, at least of the big three. From worst to best: Schweppes, Canada Dry, Seagram's. Schweppes was by far the grossest, with a syrupy faux-sugar taste. In a metacommentary on corporate consumerism, it was by far the most widely available. The Walgreens near our old apartment literally stacked overflowing cases of Schweppes in the middles of the aisles. We'd buy it in an emergency. Canada Dry was palatable enough. Seagram's was the good stuff. That could have been the taste, or it could have been marketing: The can's design was classy, a handsome silver emblazoned with the famous Seagram's logo of two horses standing on their back legs, flanking a crest with a banner beneath reading, "Integrity. Craftsmanship. Tradition." Things I believed in. But I swear it tasted crisper. For some reason, it was difficult to reliably find in stores. That was unfortunate, but that night it also gave me a much-needed mission.

Brian and I hit the streets, popping into every bodega and grocery store we passed. A head shop that had a fridge with sodas. Nothing. The newfangled, ugly grocery store. Nothing. The discount shop with bare shelves that looked disconcertingly untouched in decades. Nothing. Nothing, nothing, nothing. Forget Seagram's; there was no diet ginger ale at all. I wanted to deliver something nice for my grieving wife. She had expressed a desire, maybe her first in the time since Renzo had died, and all it would cost was $1.99 and a little bit of legwork, and I was coming up empty. We eventually did find some diet Schweppes, which I brought back like the world's biggest consolation prize. She didn't care, but I was dejected.

Allegra took great care of me, of Renzo. But she was so self-sufficient. As she began to mourn, where would I fit in?

After the immediate shock of Renzo's death, my own neediness, still undirected, was beginning to bubble up. I worried about my ability to simultaneously tend to myself and, if needed, to her. Would it be worse to be needed and not be able to deliver or to not be needed in the first place? Where would we fit into each other's lives without him? We had once before, but it was difficult to imagine those first childless years as a couple as anything other than an alternate reality. Where we were was way too real.

The day Renzo had his aneurysm, in the afternoon before it happened, I distinctly remember telling him that it was going to be a pleasure to watch him grow up. It seems ridiculous to write that here, the foreshadowing so on the nose as to be unbelievable. But it's true. To him and Allegra, I said, "I love our little family." After the struggles around his birth, job loss, the pandemic, it felt, finally, like we had made it to the other side. We had, I suppose, just not how I envisioned it.

I was dreading Brian's return to Berlin. I knew that when he left, this interim stage of our life, with Renzo's death still new enough that its reality had not fully taken hold, would end. When we vacated the Airbnb and moved into our new apartment, our future would begin. I'd have preferred if it didn't.

"Old friends" is a rare category of relationship, one free from hierarchy and tension, an ease of understanding benefiting from years of traipsing through the seasons of life together. When Brian and I moved to New York together, me from my parents' basement and him from the suburbs of Chicago, he'd only recently moved back to the U.S. from Ghana, where he'd lived for a year, supported by a Fulbright grant he'd been awarded to make a documentary about the country's rap scene. He returned with a good deal of footage, which never turned into a film. But he also brought home a suitcase full of cassette tapes he'd bought. In his bedroom, he hatched a plan to convert the tapes into MP3s and upload the music to the internet and make a blog. *Awesome Tapes from Africa,* he'd call it.

That project took over his life, eventually bringing him to Europe as a DJ, where he grew his hair and beard, got cool glasses, met his wife, and had Miles. He eventually started a record label named after his blog. Before he returned home, Brian did have one piece of business on his agenda. Though it had been a decade since he lived in New York, he still maintained a storage space in the city. He wanted to visit it, take inventory, trash the junk, and prep the rest for shipping to Germany. I said I'd go with him, even though the space was in Brooklyn Navy Yard, and to get there we'd have to cross Willoughby Avenue, the street on which I walked Renzo to and from daycare every day. No-man's-land. I drove us there, one of the last times for many months I'd cross that street unless I was in the back of a taxi, where I could close my eyes as we traversed the threshold.

The storage space was no bigger than a closet, but it contained thousands of records, stacked in a wobbly tower of milk crates. There were huge and unliftable cardboard boxes of books and CDs, and an archive-worthy number of African cassette tapes. My job was to go through the boxes of records and pull out anything that held value. Brian would hand carry those on the plane to reduce his eventual import tax bill.

Among the CDs and records from his personal collection,

Brian found several boxes of back stock from his record label, and he asked me if we could drop them off at his distributor's office in Bushwick, a Brooklyn neighborhood a short drive away. It was run by a man named Matt, whom I'd gotten to know over time through the local music scene. He runs several record labels, often painstakingly reissuing underappreciated, experimental albums, giving shine to the historically forgotten. He is also tan, tall, and handsome, with long, golden hair. He looks like a surfer. He's also very thoughtful. Once, I mentioned to him being covetous of a black denim Rollins Band jacket that was up for auction on eBay, but that I was wary of overpaying for something relatively gaudy. I ended up bidding the maximum I was comfortable with and ultimately lost the auction by a few dollars. I was disappointed, second-guessing my frugality. A few weeks later, when Matt and I met for lunch, he pulled the jacket out of a bag and handed it to me as a gift. He'd been the high bidder.

I found his combination of good looks, kindness, and deep knowledge of the avant-garde to be almost vexing. Thoughtfulness and musical obsession were the territory of short nerds like me. We didn't have anything else to trade on. If I had to compete with someone like him, I was screwed. If Matt ever noticed my envy, he never showed it. He was probably too tall to see what I was doing down there anyway.

Matt knew Brian was coming to his office with back stock but not that I was with him. Surprised, he greeted me pleasantly. Which I figured meant he did not know about Renzo. Though it had been only a little more than a week, I imagined everyone I knew would have heard through the grapevine, but alas.

I tested the waters. "Do you know . . ." I trailed off and tried again. "Have you heard?" He did not know and he had not heard. He looked at me quizzically. It was the first time I would break this news to someone in person.

"Renzo died."

Matt crumpled. Standing there in a room full of shipping supplies, he began to cry. He'd never met Renzo. It's possible he'd never even seen his photo. Was he crying for me? For himself? He had two young boys. It's possible I personified his worst fears. Not only had the Grim Reaper visited me, but I'd now become him.

This was not good. It is not a pleasant experience to make someone else cry by plainly stating the facts of your life. Harbinger of doom was not a position I wanted. I'm a friendly person. I didn't want that to go away, but I didn't know if I had a choice. Could I continue to be myself? Or would Renzo's death always speak for me?

A woman once told me that she found me to be a curious mix of high and low self-esteem, somehow simultaneously. I found this to be savagely accurate. Boiled down, my whole life had been a choice between whether to resist pain or succumb to it. Depending on my willpower, I'd vacillate between supremely sad and dishonestly chipper. Neither pole felt like an authentic self. But what was authenticity, anyway? It was as if I had been playacting these personalities, trying on extremes, but with mush at the center. If, after Renzo's death, it appeared fated that darkness would now solidify in my core, suddenly my lifelong practice of faking it seemed like an asset. I held out hope that I might someday be pierced by light. Perhaps desire was my only consistent emotion.

The Airbnb had a wooden deck in the back. We hadn't used it much, but Brian had been sneaking off to smoke weed back there, and on the morning of his flight, eager to squeeze the most out of our remaining time together, I joined him as he lit up. He was wearing a pastel blue crewneck sweatshirt, and he had a plaid scarf jauntily wrapped around his neck, like a Frenchman. My affection for him swelled in inverse correlation to my fear of his departure. Our concierge was leaving. Our new apartment was ready and we'd move in soon. The Airbnb was a way station on this fucked-up voyage. I'd soon need to tend to myself, to Allegra. As helpful, loving, and present as everyone had been, it was only our son who had died, not theirs.

I took a photo of Brian on the porch before he left, joint in mouth. I've always loved it. I actually don't mind looking at the handful of photos I took at the Airbnb, especially the ones of Allegra doing needlepoint and beadwork. In one of them, she's laughing. In most of the photos, I can see on the table the flowers a colleague had sent, a cup of tea a friend had poured for me. Detached from their context, it looks like a collection of photos from a reunion of old friends. Of a relaxing holiday getaway. People communing. Which, it's good to remember, we were.

Jayson and Stacy recommended I get to know David Kessler's work. According to *Harvard Business Review,* Kessler is "the world's foremost expert on grief." He'd worked closely with Elisabeth Kübler-Ross, who was the reigning world's foremost expert on grief before her own death in 2004. A large part of Kübler-Ross's legacy is her classification of what she calls the five stages of grief: denial, anger, bargaining, depression, and acceptance, as described in her 1969 book *On Death and Dying*. After you experience a death, she wrote, these stages can occur in any order, with one or more possibly not occurring at all. Just weeks after Renzo's death, I'd tricked myself into thinking I had jumped all the way to acceptance when really I was trying to outrun anger and depression. Bargaining hasn't been a big one for me, nor has denial. The facts have been pretty hard to ignore.

In 2019, Kessler updated Kübler-Ross's five stages with a sixth: finding meaning. He made this addition after the death of one of his two sons, who accidentally overdosed at twenty-one years old. On Kessler's website you can find all kinds of useful material. There are straightforward sections, like chapters in a handbook, called "A Loved One's Belongings," "Grief & Holidays," and "When a Child Dies."

"When a Child Dies" is a series of videos, all of which I dragged my feet on watching until Allegra urged me to. In the videos, Kessler has a gentle presence. He's grandfatherly but young, in his sixties, with a healthy head of hair. His voice is squeaky, but he speaks softly. He's wearing a dark blue vest and a turquoise button-down shirt, standing in front of a piece of abstract art and white shutters. They are closed. A green glass vase with pink flowers peeks out from the side of the screen. Very Nancy Meyers meets Mister Rogers. The presentation has the effect of making Kessler trustworthy, if anonymous. All smooth edges, no distracting elements, no sudden movements, just a nice guy, shot authoritatively in the center of the frame, talking calmly about unthinkable disaster. Welcome to the rest of your miserable life, he may as well have been saying, this nonthreatening emissary from hell broadcasting straight to my laptop.

The first video in the series is called "The Loss—the Moment Everything Changed." Kessler focuses on the "moment" part of the loss as he explains the concept of "anticipatory grief." This is the kind I did not get an opportunity to have. For your parents, your grandparents, your pets, there is a built-in expectation that they will predecease you. So you imagine their death, imagine your life without them, as that is the natural order of things. That imagining helps prepare you for the actual event, like a practice run before the big race. With a sudden death, it's the surprise that gets you. You're unprepared. You wouldn't run a marathon if you'd never taken a jog.

As I watched Kessler's videos, about a month after Renzo's death, I found myself feeling resentful toward people who had the luxury of pregrieving their loved ones. It was strange and sad to find myself not only envying but begrudging those also in mourning, these straw men against whom I measured my own level of suffering, unfairly or otherwise. On the one hand, pain is pain is pain. On the other, it's not.

Kessler seemed to be reading my mind as, partway through the first video, he broke the third wall. "We deal with so many unwanted surprises as a parent dealing with loss," he says. "It's so much more brutal. I don't have to tell you how brutal it is. You know." I do.

I've likened grieving Renzo's death to falling off a cliff. I've found that others who have mourned unexpected deaths, of any kind, have felt a similar drop. Their loved one's existence was terra firma, and then they toppled over the edge into free fall.

I'm rewatching these videos as I write this. It's eerie to see them again after a few years. Watching for the first time, I was totally bewildered, stumbling around in the dark. Kessler was describing the death world like a store manager showing me the ropes on my first day on the job. Now I've been working there for a long time. I know where everything is.

Kessler describes a moment not too long after his son died when, at a birthday party, a loose acquaintance turned to him and asked, "How are the boys?" Boys, plural. The boys were no longer plural. It was not, however, the right time to explain. He begged off the question, said they had a lot to catch up on and that he'd call the next day to explain. "Your story," he says to the camera, "is yours to tell or not."

I found this comforting. I find it difficult to lie, even by omission. How would I answer basic questions, the same ones I often asked of people? "Do you have any children?" Did I anymore? Kessler's approach gave me permission to do what needed to be done in order to cope.

Once, while leaving a restaurant a few months after Renzo's death, I ran into a former co-worker I hadn't seen in a long time. "How's your son?" she asked as I shuffled sideways between tables on my way out the door. I did not want to get into it. "He's good," I said. That was not what I meant. I tried to correct myself. "He's, uh . . ." She looked at me quizzically. "I'll text you," I said. I was horrified with myself for saying he was good. It felt like blasphemy. But when I got home, I texted her and explained. It was better than crying in the middle of the restaurant. It was the first time I felt like something could have been worse.

Grief has rules, Kessler explains in the second video. He likens it to blindness or the loss of a limb. You have to learn to navigate this new terrain. He spends a while talking about laughter. Is laughing disloyal? No, it's not. Social media, he says, bringing with it many photos of other people's obliviously happy families, can be a risk; be mindful. And don't expect your spouse to be your support system; they are as out of gas as you. This was ominous. "How can two empty tanks support each other?"

A number of times he refers to the pitfalls of conversations with strangers in the checkout line. (I wondered if he had not yet discovered online shopping.) People will disappoint you; be prepared. "People say stupid things in life, and they don't quit saying them in grief." He says it out the side of his mouth in a funny, conspiratorial kind of way, like a stand-up comic.

Surprisingly, he starts off the third video with a joke that seems more for the grief counselors' group text than for the newly bereaved. "People always ask me, 'How long will I grieve?' I say, 'How long will your child be dead?'"

But as the video goes on, he regains his seriousness. "The goal of grief work is to remember our child with more love than pain." I dreaded this idea. The pain I felt mourning Renzo's death was evidence of his existence. Missing him was the closest I could get to being with him. The worse I felt, the truer our love. The better I'd begin to feel, the further he'd fade. Time moves in only one direction: the wrong one. "No one wants to be the bereaved parent," Kessler says. But "we've been given more life. So what are we going to do with the rest of our lives?"

It reminded me of two lines from Mary Oliver's poem "Poem 133: The Summer Day" that have been so oft quoted as to become cliché.

> Tell me, what is it you plan to do
> with your one wild and precious life?

What so many saw as an invitation I now saw as a threat. *Tell me.*

I'd never read the entire poem, and so I sought it out. I was not surprised to find out that most of it is about Oliver traipsing through the grass, appreciating the anatomy of a grasshopper. I was, however, surprised to see that the line before those famous final two is "Doesn't everything die at last, and too soon?"

If Kessler was right, I had a choice to make about how to use the time I'd been given. He said I should live in a way that honored Renzo. How would I do that? Always have smoothies? Never have a smoothie again? It seemed there were no right answers, only wrong ones.

When, in 2010, the writer Sheila Heti wrote a buzzed-about book, *How Should a Person Be?,* I rushed to get a copy. The title articulated the only question I've ever felt was worth asking. If there was any conversation to be had, it should be about this. The book was good, but I couldn't wrap my head around it. It wasn't that the writing or ideas were bad; it was that they were there at all. Any attempt to actually answer the title's question felt like a waste of time. The book should have been blank. Once you behold an orb, you don't crack it open to see what's inside.

Years after it happened, I now realized the reason being laid off during the pandemic had been so difficult. My job at *Pitchfork* had defined my life for me, no questions asked. I didn't have to interrogate myself any further. I liked music, I liked writing, I liked editing, I liked people. Here I was, an editor at a music publication. It was a dummy-proof identity. It allowed me to not have to consider who I really wanted to be. The fact that I didn't really like it that much was beside the point.

One thing I did know about myself was that I'd always wanted to be a parent. I love kids. They're excitable, they're weird, they love to shove food in their mouths and make big messes and not clean them up. They remind me of myself. Devoting myself to a child of my own seemed like an ideal scenario in which to disappear. And it was. Renzo's life served to define my own in a way that felt much healthier than my relationship with work. While some of this was emotional, a lot of it was logistical. He was a baby; he had to be watched at every moment. It was exhausting but euphoric.

So when he died, I was left with the big question of how my one wild and precious life should be. My temporary job at Vice had turned permanent, and I'd taken a leave of absence. My boss was understanding and urged me to forget about my responsibilities there, and so I did. That left Allegra and me with, for the first time in nearly two years, unoccupied days. After the shivah and Brian's departure, the stream of people in and out of our home and lives slowed. Free time, once precious and now ample, was a menace. Renzo's life had stopped; ours had not. Kessler had given us a guide, but it was for the toughest moments. Experiencing the worst would be rare. Even if we went to one of Kessler's grief retreats, we'd still have to go home a week later.

We needed, at least, to unpack. The living room of our new apartment was filled with boxes from the moving company, Piece of Cake, their logo of snapping fingers printed in pink on the sides. Friends and family had packed our old apartment for us. Because Allegra and I had not been able to do our own purge before moving, each box contained an odd array of things, necessities nestled beside stuff we probably would have gotten rid of. My deodorant in a plastic bag with a collection of seashells. A box of USB drives and kitchen knives. Pens taken from every restaurant I'd ever eaten at. A salt lamp. Looking through our own belongings was like browsing through an estate sale.

All of Renzo's things had been moved to Allegra's parents' house. We kept with us one stuffed bear that he had cherished. He sat on Allegra's nightstand and I'd greet him when he caught my eye.

We took it slow, as we were taking everything. What furniture we did have was for our previous, smaller apartment, so the new place had the feeling of a shrunken dollhouse. I liked the apartment, though. A corner unit, the living room flooded with light in the late afternoon. "Change is good," people say, which is obviously total bullshit, but maybe some change, the tiniest fraction of an iota, could be passable.

Jayson had become close with Kessler, and he offered to introduce us. We took him up on it, and he connected us over email. Kessler responded quickly. He said he was willing to talk.

"My heart sank when I read about your sweet son Renzo. Would Thursday, January 13th at 6 PM EST work for you?"

It would. His assistant sent us a Zoom link.

For a brief time, Allegra and I had the living room set up backward from how it is now, with the couch where the chairs are now and the chairs where the couch is. So when I remember our conversation with Kessler, the two of us on the couch together, huddled over my laptop, the memory feels inverted, wrong. We should have been facing the other way.

I had high hopes for our bespoke treatment. Once he heard our story, I imagined, Kessler would have some silver bullet to decimate our grief. Everyone grieves differently, he'd said in his videos. Now was the time for him to see how we did it. And then fix it.

Kessler was warm and patient, but most of what he said was the same as in his videos. The one addition was that he kept telling us to be resilient. *That's it? That's the big secret?* We'd climbed the mountain, seen the oracle, and he was out of ideas.

I know now it's not anyone's fault. Certainly not Kessler's. He had done more than anyone to help us heal in those early days from that for which there is no cure. But if even he had nothing for us other than "resilience," it was difficult to not feel hopeless. We made plans to check in and talk again but never did.

I decided I'd try attending a meeting of the Compassionate Friends, a support group for parents who have lost children. Kessler had discussed the power of hearing the stories of other parents whose children had died years prior, to understand how life might look eventually. I felt that ease of understanding in the presence of Jayson and Stacy. If there were other parents with life lessons to offer, I'd readily accept them.

Compassionate Friends was run as a network of independent regional groups. They'd largely moved online during the pandemic. To avoid the presence of trolls, an unfortunately common side effect of posting public Zoom links, you had to register for a meeting via a form on their website, explaining your loss. I filled it out, writing dispassionately about Renzo and his death. It was not the fault of the organization, but I felt resentful. Both resentful that I needed to prove my status as a bereaved parent and resentful that I was a bereaved parent in the first place. As if the form sensed this animosity, after I clicked the Submit button, nothing happened. I tried several times to submit it to no avail. The New York branch of Compassionate Friends appeared to be a small organization, so I figured I could take a screenshot of my information and send it to the administrator in lieu of a properly submitted form. He emailed me back and thanked me and noted that "few members would know how to screen capture."

I was not heartened by this observation. Who was going to this meeting that didn't know how to take a screenshot? I imagined myself in conversation with a roomful of people decades my senior, discussing the long-ago deaths of their children, as well as their befuddlement with commonplace technology. I imagined further alienation, not understanding.

The Compassionate Friends administrator also mentioned to me that I did not fill out Renzo's birthday or date of death, as asked for. I'd omitted them on purpose. It felt too intimate to share. He said it was not required, but that "we use them to be able to list Our children in the newsletter in the month in which the significant date occurs." I don't know if the capital O was a typo or not, but I hated it. Our children. Renzo was mine.

I did not attend the meeting.

Eventually, through mutual friends, I was introduced to a man named Matt, who had also lost his young son, Lionel. Lionel had died five years earlier of SUDC, or sudden unexplained death in childhood (similar to SIDS, which occurs in children under one). Matt had an older son, Calvin, and a younger daughter, Alma, who had been born fifteen months after Lionel's death.

Matt was a comedy TV writer. I was nervous to ask for help from someone who was paid to be funny. I texted instead of calling.

I lost my son last month very suddenly. I understand something similar happened to you. I'm very sorry. If you have some time to talk, I'd be grateful to hear about your experience and where you are now.

I'd not realized Matt lived in Los Angeles, where it was early morning. He responded a half hour later. "I'm really, really sorry man. Hearing your story really sent me back to all of those feelings I'm sure you're feeling now, which are impossible to articulate to anyone who hasn't gone through this."

I felt immediate relief. He understood. I felt sad, too. Sad for him, that I'd brought him back to such a horrible time, and sad that this was what was going to count as camaraderie.

He called me and I paced around our new bedroom while I told him about Renzo. I talked to him about Renzo's middle name. Matt knew who Henry Rollins was, which made me feel like he knew who I was.

We were on the phone for an hour. Matt told me about the time after Lionel died, which, for him and his wife, included a lot of walking. Logistical questions filled my brain. How could they afford to be off work for months? What did they talk about on the walks? Who was watching their living son while they walked? Did they get in the car and go to faraway places? LA isn't really a walking city.

But I didn't ask anything. I wanted him to go at his own pace, for him to decide what was important. Within months of Lionel's death, Matt said, he and his wife agreed they wanted their family to be four again, and set out to have another child. He explained how they had solicited donations to build a playground in Lionel's honor, how they go to the mountains every year on his birthday. Then he told me something Calvin, his older son, said that remains one of the truest expressions of the collision between bereavement and real life I have heard.

Shortly after Lionel died, Matt explained, he and his wife took Calvin to Griffith Observatory. Except they couldn't find parking. All the lots were full and they kept being turned away by the attendants. It was getting frustrating. From the back seat, Calvin piped up. "Can't we just tell them my brother died?"

It made sense. They'd been through enough. The world should give them VIP access to whatever they wanted, convenient parking the barest of minimums. Instead, they had to keep driving.

I greatly identified with this childhood logic. It was the opposite of the gentle approach Kessler urged, the need to keep the truth for quieter moments. Calvin wanted to use the truth like a battering ram. And that's what the truth felt like, knocking around in my guts. If pain burned in me all the time, shouldn't everyone else be a little bit on fire too? If you can't bring back my dead son, can you at least give me a decent parking space?

Despite my capriciousness in regard to accepting the wisdom and advice of others, I continued seeking it out. I've always looked for guides, gurus, in times of difficulty, hoping they'd offer a vista into another, better way of life. I was reading whatever I could, my antennae up for transmissions of wisdom. Online, I stumbled across the audio recording of an interview Toni Morrison gave to *The Paris Review* in 1993. One thing she said was "I think of beauty as an absolute necessity. I don't think it's a privilege or an indulgence. It's not even a quest. I think it's almost like knowledge, which is to say, it's what we were born for. I think finding, incorporating, and then representing beauty is what humans do." This quote, surfaced years after the original interview, when the entire unedited conversation was turned into a podcast, was not included in the original print interview; it must have been edited out. Why? Too moony? Too frivolous? Perhaps, but this was the first bit of insight that truly made me reconsider what I'd need to do in order to heal.

I'd never lived the life of an aesthete, but I was suddenly starved for beauty. Without Renzo's pure presence, it was like I'd become beauty anemic and I needed to over-index in order to even approach neutral.

My usual sources were running dry. Music had become an albatross. Even my ears were grieving. I'd put on a record and recoil. Everything suddenly sounded sour. I was an idiot for ever having liked techno, unfeeling and inhuman. Indie rock felt whiny and immature. Jazz, an interminable screed of noisomeness. Hardcore was the music of belligerent blowhards. Bill Callahan's was the only singing voice I could handle. He advised me well in his guttural drawl. "No matter how far wrong you've gone / You can always turn around." But after weeks of nonstop Callahan, I needed to find diversity in sages.

Before he left, Brian had given me a few records from his storage space, including an album of Indian santour music. A santour, I learned, is essentially a hammer dulcimer, a stringed instrument played with tiny mallets. Imagine someone strumming the high notes of a harp at a warp speed. Giving Callahan a break, I listened to the santour. The songs were long and open, unstructured but soft, with no dissonance and no words. When the santour played, it sounded like the room was glowing. Beauty, finally beheld.

Unfortunately, it's difficult to locate santour records in America, so after dozens of plays of my sole recording, I did finally have to move on. I explored different pianists, looking for music that was close to imperceptible. I discovered an album of piano music literally called *Walk in Beauty.* The music was gentle, like snow falling. Then I started spending a lot of time with music by the pianist Bill Evans. His albums were often gently elegiac, as though he knew, when he recorded them more than half a century earlier, that I'd one day need them. One song I gravitated toward, a solo piece performed in 1966 at New York's Town Hall, was dedicated to Evans's father after his then-recent death. Long and laconic, it was not a lament, nor was it a celebration. It was a recitation of facts, of pain, of admiration, and of love, translated into music and banged out on the keys.

I started going to record stores to buy every Bill Evans record I could find. A second-floor shop in Chinatown that specialized in Japanese music for some reason contained a bounty. *Undercurrent, Explorations, Conversations with Myself, Alone, You Must Believe in Spring.* I played each album over and over until its songs were a part of me, and then I'd get a new one and begin the process again. As I delved deeper into the back half of Evans's career, the portraits on the albums' covers got increasingly haggard. He went from handsome and clean-shaven in the fifties and sixties to sallow, hunched, and skinny in the seventies—his body rotting away from the effects of heroin use. In 1980, Evans, in New York to perform a series of gigs, died from a fatal hemorrhage at fifty-one after a lifetime of drug and alcohol abuse. A tragedy. He was so young, depending on how you look at it.

Though it was recorded in 1977, *You Must Believe in Spring* wasn't released until after Evans died. It's a playful record that includes a recording of "Freddie Freeloader" from Miles Davis's landmark 1959 album *Kind of Blue,* on which Evans was the pianist. I wonder if he recorded it again, almost twenty years later, to remind everyone, or maybe himself, of his presence in history. It's a jaunty rendition, one loosened by time. Elsewhere on the album, Evans covers the *M*A*S*H* theme, also known as "Suicide Is Painless." I tried not to get any ideas.

Renzo, of course, died on the wintriest day, Christmas Eve. Thinking of his cold-weather death, I liked the idea of believing in spring and not summer, the hedonist's season. Spring is a reasonable time of year. On its face, believing in spring doesn't promise much other than a realist's acknowledgment of the change of season. A reckoning with the inevitable passage of time, a reckoning with which I was struggling. Spring would come, a fact; believing in its renewal was up to me.

We continued unpacking. Records were alphabetized. Books were shelved according to various overlapping methods: size, subject matter, color. We unrolled the red Turkish rug that had belonged to my grandmother, then my parents, then me, then Allegra and me. There are photos of my sister and me lying on it as babies, twin blobs, and, nearly forty years later, of Renzo lying on it, too.

One evening friends came over to eat pizza and help empty the last of the unopened moving boxes. I ignored them and opened a huge black plastic bag full of change and for hours sorted the coins into wrappers, standing in the corner of the kitchen. I'd read about valuable old pennies, so after I sorted them out from the quarters, nickels, and dimes, I examined each one for age and other variations. I watched several amateur YouTube videos on my phone about what to look for, but nothing we had was worth anything.

Most of what we needed to put away was clothes. Over time, I'd amassed a large collection of band T-shirts, many for metal bands with names like Cryptopsy and Suffocation. I'd enjoyed wearing them, with their cartoonish and orgiastic scenes of suffering. Despite all the blood and skeletons, they were more playful than violent. My Napalm Death shirt, with impaled people with their faces shredded to the bone. Or Cannibal Corpse, with a skeleton eating his own entrails. But where I had once found humor, I now found disgust. Not at the grotesquerie itself but at these bands' belief that they had any right to depict the horrors of death. The singer for Cannibal Corpse, a man who'd nicknamed himself Corpsegrinder, was well known for being a lover of Disney World.

Grief was a black desert. He held no claim to true pain; he lived in Florida and his real name was George. This pantomime of pain suddenly outraged me. So I gave away all my metal T-shirts to my friends that night, save one, my Morbid Angel shirt. It was comparatively tasteful, plain black with their red logo printed in miniature just over my heart.

Once we settled in, at the suggestion of many people, Allegra and I did yoga. We set up two mats side by side on the Turkish rug. I've done yoga on and off at various points in my life, but I'd never done it at home. Dean had recommended the YouTube series *Yoga with Adriene,* and so Allegra and I set up a laptop on a kitchen stool. It was January, and to welcome the new year, Adriene was releasing one new video each day for her "MOVE—a 30 Day Yoga Journey" series. We committed to a month of daily practice. I liked that it was current; I felt a part of something larger than myself. One friend said her mom, back home in Minneapolis, was doing the videos each day, too. Dean wanted to join us, so, most days, we'd do a screen share on Zoom. He'd do yoga on his bedroom floor beside his chocolate Lab, Flaco, who was flopped on the bed, uninterested in the whole thing.

Adriene proved to be a benevolent presence. A Texan, she spoke with a slight drawl. In most of the videos, filmed in an airy loft, her dog, a handsome blue heeler named Benji, lay beside her, Flaco's recumbent kin. Adriene, from time to time, between stretches, would pet Benji. I envied both dogs' simple peace.

Adriene began each episode with a warm welcome and ended each with an encouraging goodbye. Her signature greeting: "Hop into something comfy and let's get started." I did as she said. Yoga is one of the few things I can do without glasses. I liked the effect of being present while the world was blurry.

At the end of day nine's video, "Curiosity," Adriene, flat on her back in Savasana, with her hand on her lower abdomen and Benji at her feet, invited us to explore. "If there's anything you'd like to do here with your body before you step off the mat, take the time," she said. "Listen, and stay curious." I appreciated the sentiment. I wanted to do that. I wanted to be resilient. I wanted to take the advice I was being given and go out into the world with it, but I was so tired. I was sad and I was angry and I knew I would be for a long time. But I imagined that, one day, I would no longer want to be.

Despite largely feeling like garbage, I did have to go back to work. I returned on a Friday, hoping a one-day workweek would be a modest reintroduction.

In the early months of 2022 we were all still working from home, though it would be only a few months before the big push for return to office. I set up my laptop at the desk in the corner of our living room. I was eager to demonstrate to my colleagues that I was still in the mix, that I was still a valid leader for my small team. I began sending messages in our various chat rooms. I imagined everyone would welcome me back and treat me with deference, but I discovered there had been a power struggle in my absence, and some colleagues met my return grudgingly. This bewildered me because not only did it feel heartless, it felt stupid. Who cared about power? Who cared about jobs? Should we not all support one another until we clocked out and collapsed?

Over the next few weeks, one of my co-workers checked in on me regularly, which at first felt like kindness but later felt like keeping tabs. One day, when I disappeared from the computer for some time, she was persistent in texting to ask if I was okay.

I was fine, but the truth is that I was at a coffee shop, doing a job interview. After returning to such a tense dynamic, I hoped to make a change. I knew the woman I was interviewing with through a mutual friend, and I knew she knew about Renzo. As soon as she saw me she cried. My presence was enough to break her. In turn, I was steely. I'd dressed up for this. I offered her tissues from my coat pocket. I spoke at length, with as much focus as I could muster, about my employment history and my attitude toward people management. If she cried, I told myself, I had to get the job. That was the rightful exchange. But I didn't. They said I wasn't the right fit. Misfortune, I learned, is not a professional qualification.

That afternoon, after the interview, I met a former colleague at another coffee shop, a quirky spot that had pink and purple furniture and served vegan empanadas. I was glad to hear from this guy, whom I liked and found funny. Despite the circumstance, I was happy to reconnect. But the conversation was odd. It was clear he didn't know what to say, which I didn't mind, but instead of being stricken, he was blabbering. Eventually, he asked me if I wanted to have another child, which I thought was a fairly forward question. But I'd been asked and so I answered. Yes, I did, very much. Allegra and I were in agreement. We couldn't imagine life not as parents. David Kessler—and everyone else—would tell us we were *still* parents, but we knew the difference. We were not. Saying we were still parents felt like a purposeful denial of Renzo's death, not an acknowledgment of his life. We were not parents. We were something else.

Then he said something I did not expect. "That's gonna be the saddest boner in the world," he said.

In the moment, I barely responded. I may have even faux laughed so he didn't feel bad. I wanted to move on as soon as possible. I wanted it to not have happened. People said a lot of weird shit to me after Renzo died, but this was by far the weirdest.

Why? Why did they keep doing that? At the time, every bizarre pawing at sympathy felt like adding insult to injury, like salt on a very much still open wound. Was conveying simple and genuine condolences so hard?

I think the answer for a lot of people was yes, it was. By definition, all death is an obliteration. Any bystander to loss of life is going to feel the erosion of solid ground. If you're already an odd person, as many of my friends were, you're not going to suddenly become extra normal, with a clear-eyed understanding of how to dole out comfort. What you're going to do is say some weird shit. I get that now. I didn't at the time. It's taken me years to even begin to understand the magnitude of Renzo's loss. Literally, I had to write this book. I can't expect someone else to have understood that over the course of an afternoon.

The writers, musicians, and yoga instructors I sought out in the weeks after Renzo's death all gave me solace precisely because they weren't my friends or my family. They weren't talking to or about me. I was not sitting across the table from them while they flailed around. If I wanted to find value in someone's song or book, to apply it to my situation, that was my own decision. It was not a conversation. That had ups and it had downs. Adriene was not my friend. She might not have been able to give me a hug through the computer, but she also wouldn't say any sad-boner stuff. If Bill Callahan talked about betting on horses and I wanted to hear a healing narrative, great. With real people with real faults, I was sometimes strong enough to offer grace; other times I was not. I wanted companionship and insight, but I wanted them on my terms. I know that's not how things work, but I continued to seek it out. I tried to imagine what I would do if I could do anything. Who could I talk to that would help me heal?

Henry Rollins, I realized with the total clarity of the deluded and desperate. He'd gotten me through one crisis; he could get me through another. I fantasized about spending the day with him. I imagined myself flying to California, going to lunch with him, driving around and looking out the car window while he shouted hoarse aphorisms that would magically cure me. I don't know what I intended to ask him. The meaning of life? I know now how absurd this seems, that a stranger might offer me more insight into my own life than my friends and family could offer me, than I could offer myself, but at that moment my conviction that he could fix me was unwavering. I think I was just tapped out.

So I asked my boss if she would send me to LA to interview Rollins. We priced out the cost of a reporting trip, a few days in a hotel, a rental car, and round-trip coach tickets. It was in the budget. A harebrained scheme, but she said to go for it, an act of support and generosity I did not discount. I found Rollins's publicist's email address on his website and sent a note. I tried to sound convincing, if a little desperate, which I was.

> Hello
>
> My name is Matthew, I'm writing with a press request for Henry Rollins for Vice. The influence Henry has had on my life, his passion, his individualism, his humor, and I think his grace, has largely shaped who I am and, I hoped, my son. And in many ways, it did, until he died suddenly in December of a rare condition called AVM that was found in his brain. Like Henry, Renzo was charming and funny, a little wild, and curious. He was 22 months old.
>
> Things have been tough as my wife and I search for, if not answers, purpose. We've spoken to all manner of people, from a rabbi to grief counselors, friends, other bereaved parents. But I hoped I might be able to speak with Henry, to hear his thoughts on life, loss, purpose, purposelessness. I would write a piece based on our conversation/s. Let me know what you think. I am happy to discuss further on email or over the phone. Thank you
>
> Best
> Matthew

I quickly received a response from Henry himself. He said he wanted to help, but that he couldn't. "Respectfully," he wrote, "I don't want any presence whatsoever in the contentsphere of Vice." This was not the first time a principled punk-rock elder had rejected an interview request of mine on the basis of its being for Vice. It was a troublesome company with a legacy of sexism. I was embarrassed. I asked him if he'd be open to my writing a piece if it was published elsewhere. With some limitations, he said. This led to a brief back-and-forth about what constituted a "print" publication. "When you get a chance," he said, "let me know your thoughts."

"I'll think about what makes sense for this idea and get back to you soon," I responded. In my email I attached two photos of Renzo. In one, he'd just gotten his hair cut. Renzo was a happy boy, but the few times he'd had his hair cut had terrified him. Allegra had gone the first time or two, but he screamed and cried so much that it rattled her, and she asked me to take him alone for what was his final cut. The hairdresser, a hoarse grandmother who said she had been cutting hair for decades, was unfazed by his howling. I, however, was fazed. When she finished, I was in such a rush to get him out of there that we made it several blocks before I realized I hadn't even strapped him into the stroller. It was a nice day out and we went to meet Allegra in the park. When we arrived, Allegra was standing near the park entrance, chatting with friends. We took Renzo out and everyone admired his new look. As a gesture of goodwill, the barber had given him an orange balloon, and in the photo he's holding it, looking up at the camera. He looks so incredibly handsome.

In the other photo I sent, Renzo is sitting in his high chair, holding an LP by the jazz musician Don Cherry. I thought this one might appeal to Henry, a noted record collector with a vast appreciation for music. I wanted him to see who I had been raising. His namesake.

"Beautiful boy," Rollins replied.

I had been dreading Renzo's second birthday. February 6. It would be the last time we'd have a milestone of his until the anniversary of his death the following winter, which was a mixed blessing. So much time. We were not ready to celebrate, which felt unfair to him, but punishing ourselves with abject misery didn't feel right either. Distraction seemed like the only way we would make it through the day.

Allegra and I made plans with Dean and his wife, Bela. In the morning, we got pedicures. I'd never had one. I enjoyed the paraffin wax eating away the dead skin on my heel. Then we went to their apartment and ordered pizza. Dean had recently purchased Bela a red-light therapy mask, and we all took turns wearing it and taking photos. It made us look like satanic hockey goalies. We watched reality TV and I fell asleep on the couch, spooning Flaco the dog. It was a fine day. My dread had been misplaced. I missed Renzo, but no more than any day before or after. It turned out there was no way this one day could be worse than any other. Infinity plus one isn't a thing.

How would this change over time? I was eager to keep hearing from those who'd experienced great and sudden loss how they had survived. Like my friend Sam.

On Christmas Eve of 2012, ten years to the day before Renzo died, Sam's mother, Prudence, was murdered. She was a teacher who'd grown up in New Zealand before moving to the U.S., where she had Sam, his sister, and later their half sister. Prudence had been dating a man she met at the gym. After they'd broken up, he arrived at her house unannounced, and he struck her. Sam's half sister found her mother unconscious in front of their house. She died soon after. This was in Seattle, where Sam grew up. At the time of her death, he was on the other side of the country, at home, in New York.

Sam's then girlfriend called to tell me the news. Sam and I worked together at the music magazine, and we were close friends from the years we'd spent sitting side by side at a desk in our overcrowded office. Because it was Christmas, we were off work for the holiday break. Sam would return to Seattle, but not yet. I asked if I could come visit. His girlfriend said yes.

Sam lived with two roommates in a big two-story apartment in South Williamsburg, Brooklyn. When I arrived, it was full of friends. I brought him a bottle of booze. Sam was in good spirits. I stayed for a few hours and we talked, mostly about music, which is what we usually talked about. His mom and her death did not come up.

When we returned to work in the new year, I told the staff what had happened. They cried. Sam had asked for the first day after the holidays off so he wouldn't be there when they all found out. He came in that next day and, like he always did, got to work.

Over the course of the next year, Sam made a major, conscious change in his life: Every day, on his lunch break, he would walk across the street to the gym and run on the treadmill for an hour. He'd take a shower and come back to the office. Over time, his body slimmed, tautened. Not an unnatural amount, but you could see he was different.

We never talked much about what happened to his mom. We did our work and talked about music. The school where she taught had a big memorial ceremony, which he said felt strange. This was a whole other part of her life to which he had no access. She and his father were divorced; his relationship with her was tough at times. He kept me up to date about the court dates for the man who killed her, who was eventually sentenced to thirty years in prison.

About a year after his mother's death, Sam quit to go freelance. He wanted to see what it would be like to try to make it on his own. I did not expect that we would grow closer in the years following his departure from the magazine. After his mother's death, Sam, who had always been a bit tough, became truly warm. He met and married a funny and kind woman, and they had a son. Like me, Sam had always wanted to be a dad. He was good at it, too. Though he was two years younger than me, a crucial difference in our early twenties, that divide eroded. I began to look up to him. I wanted the serenity he exuded. When he moved from New York to Los Angeles, I was crushed. We stayed in touch, texting often about our young families.

Sam came to visit in early spring, four months after Renzo died. When he arrived, I asked him what he wanted to do. I was tired of having to figure it out myself. He said he wanted to go shopping. That sounded good to me. We took the subway to Chinatown and went to bookstores and record stores, putzed around the city. We walked to SoHo to visit a clothing store Sam liked. Cool teens were skateboarding outside. I felt a million years old. Sam tried on baggy pants. I took a photo and sent it to his wife for her approval. She said he didn't need any more pants. I encouraged him to buy them anyway, for vicarious retail therapy, and he did. He bought so many books they couldn't fit in his suitcase and I later had to mail them to him in a big box.

The day before he left, Sam and I sat in the living room so we could talk. Sudden death on Christmas Eve; what are the odds? I was surprised when Sam's mom died that he didn't want to talk about it, but I understood now. Maybe he was in shock. Maybe he was angry. Whatever the reason, he wasn't ready. It takes so much to be ready. I remembered being in his living room, baffled about what to say to him. Now he was in mine, telling me what I needed to hear.

"Ask me anything," he said. What I wanted to know most was what my future would look like. Sam had lost his mother, not his child. It wasn't parallel. But it wasn't far off.

"How often do you think about your mom?" I asked. He

said not that much. He didn't lament this as tragic or celebrate it as evolved. It had been a decade since her death. He said the frequency with which thoughts of his mother crossed his mind wasn't bad, it wasn't good, it just was. He didn't blame himself. Nor should he. But I worried that I would punish myself as Renzo's memory slipped away. I was scared my connection to him would fade. I knew it would. I was looking for permission to accept the inevitable.

I'd asked Jayson and Stacy the same thing that day in the park. Did they think about Greta every day? No, they said. I think I went cross-eyed. Renzo was alive so briefly and the future was so long. The rest of my life would likely contain the length of his dozens of times over. What place would his twenty-two months hold in my life as the years wore on? What would I remember? What could I stand to forget?

As Sam and I talked, the sun started flooding the living room, as I was learning it did in the midafternoons. I could see the dust particles floating in the air. Sam was sitting on the velvety blue easy chair Renzo had liked. "Blue chair," he would say toward the end of his life, when he finally had the words, when he wanted a boost. He'd sit on my lap while we read books there. Would I forget that?

With the exception of that living room conversation, Sam's trip ended up not being about explicating grief. Unlike with most people, I did not feel like I had to illustrate my pain to him. He had been there. Instead, his trip was about having fun. I was beginning to learn that fun was its own singular experience, different from happiness. I wasn't happy. Not even close. But I could still try to have a good time.

Allegra and I decided to go on a vacation in the spring. Her brother works in the hotel business and got us a substantial discount at a nice place in Miami. Our room was large, with a balcony overlooking Collins Avenue. It was the beginning of Passover, and a huge portion of the hotel's private beach was roped off for an outdoor seder. We sat beside a billowing tent staked in the sand. In the distant ocean we could see what looked like a huge oil tanker. Behind us, some guy was listening to music on a portable speaker, playing some of the worst music I've ever heard in my life. Even Allegra could not muster generosity. Terrible music became a theme of the trip, as the next day, when we moved to sit poolside on the rooftop, a DJ was blasting EDM remixes of classic rock, an idea so heinous it was almost diabolical. Simon and Garfunkel: "Hello darkness my old *friend, friend, friend, friend, friend, friend.*" The Doors: "Riders on the *storm, storm, storm, storm.*" I wish I were making this up.

We pushed through. It was good to be in the sun. We read and swam all day. A French couple drank champagne, their feet dangling in the water. A chubby guy with a fat gold ring, a Crypto.com hat, and a bushy mustache was standing in the shallow end, soaking it all in. He was having the time of his life. Everyone there was. No one knew us or why we were there. No one cared. We were tourists like everyone else.

Allegra loves pools and I love watching her swim. As she treaded water, her long hair floated behind her on the surface. She looked like a mermaid. If you're going to be sad, you might as well be sad in a pool.

At lunch, lounging, Allegra and I talked about how we had tried once to bring Renzo into a pool; he hated it. He was happier on dry land. Probably because the first time we tried to coerce him into a body of water, at the beach on Cape Cod, on a very hot day, we inconsiderately dunked his lower half. We had not thought to ease him in.

Renzo was always on my mind, but in a way that hovered, cloudlike, over all other thoughts. Talking about this memory, recounting it as a tidy narrative, was different. It was the first time we'd gotten close to doing anything like "reminiscing."

Friends bought Allegra and me a gift certificate to the hotel's spa. We both made appointments for massages, but they would only give one to me, because Allegra was pregnant. No massages for anyone in the first trimester. We'd only found out about a month before. The woman at the front desk of the spa was one of the first people to know.

Instead of a massage they said they could give Allegra a facial, so she got two.

By the third day of the trip, she was wiped out. We had a dinner reservation, but we canceled it and ordered pizza instead. Allegra watched a Harry Potter movie while I read *The Candy House* by Jennifer Egan. It was the first time since Renzo died that I was able to concentrate enough to read a book. The book was loosely about people being able to upload their memories to a central server where others could tap in and watch. It was sci-fi, but it was also about aging, legacy, identity. It was gripping. I was happy to immerse myself in something, have a novel take me somewhere else. Probably the same reason Allegra wanted to watch Harry Potter.

The pizza arrived and we ate it on the balcony. It tasted fine, good enough. Then we heard a loud noise and looked down to see a car careening across the four-lane road, coming to a crooked stop along the double yellow lines. The driver tried in vain to get the car moving, eventually giving up, abandoning the car, and retreating to the hotel lobby across the street. Allegra went back inside to finish the movie.

I wanted to see how the scene would play out. I stayed on the balcony and watched as traffic slowed. People were honking and going nuts. Eventually, a tow truck arrived. "The tow truck is here!" I called to Allegra. She laughed at me, but she still came out to see. The sun went down. "Goodbye, sun," I said aloud for some reason, then realized what a homophonic Freudian slip I'd made. How trite. No elegance in this day's mourning. Miami made everything corny.

Though we'd both agreed in principle that we wanted to have another baby, there had been some back-and-forth about when. I wanted more time, Allegra less. She was worried. Worried that it would take a long time for her to get pregnant, worried that she might have a miscarriage and we'd have to start again.

Shortly after Renzo's death, Allegra made an appointment with a pediatric geneticist. Could what happened to him have been genetic? I'd avoided learning anything new about AVMs after we left the hospital. Any further details were a crippling reminder of his suffering. In this case, knowledge was not power. But the one valuable thing I had learned was that his condition was not believed to have been inherited. "It was a lightning strike" was how one doctor put it plainly. According to the U.S. government, an average of twenty-eight people in the country die each year from lightning strikes.

At the appointment, when asked, Allegra and I confirmed that there was no chance we were related. I was miserable in the office, swaddled in my winter coat, hoping to get out of there as soon as possible. I'd ostensibly gone to support Allegra, but my recalcitrance was making it worse. We'd done genetic testing before Renzo's birth. Allegra and I were not common carriers of anything. The doctor was now suggesting a new round, before we tried to have another child, as the testing had advanced. Hundreds of new genes could now be sequenced, annotated. What would this round of testing tell us, two years later? Nothing, it turns out. There were still no signs of anything. The doctor said we could proceed at our own risk.

Still, I wasn't ready. Not that I thought I'd ever be healed, but this was still too raw. It had only been a couple of months. If this new child's birthday was in nine months, it would be close to the anniversary of Renzo's death. If we waited longer, Allegra said, it would be close to his birthday. Time was not a safe haven. But she agreed to wait.

Then, one day, as we were sitting next to each other at our kitchen counter, she cried. Waiting was causing her so much pain. Time, when laid out like a miserable horizon, was bearing down on her. How could I participate in making anything worse for this person whom I loved? I relented, and soon Allegra was pregnant.

Nine months is an unhelpful amount of time, both too short and too long. I could imagine someone proactively becoming an entirely new person in nine months, but not me. I evolved glacially. But I knew I'd be foolish to not attempt to quicken the pace of my healing. The death of my first child was not the fault of my second. I did not want to be a bad parent. If I did not learn from my grief, I knew it would fester.

In his book *Finding Meaning,* Kessler says the best way to recover is to live with purpose. "Those who are able to find meaning tend to have a much easier time grieving than those who don't," he writes. "They're less likely to remain stuck in one of the five stages. For those who do get stuck, this can manifest in many different ways, including sudden weight gain (or loss), drug or alcohol addiction, unresolved anger, or an inability to form or commit to a new relationship out of fear of experiencing yet another loss."

I almost wished I were into drugs. But since Renzo died, I had become unable to stop eating sweets, which, as a middle-aged Jewish man who was already short and bald, put me on a collision course with nonstop George Costanza references I hoped to avoid. (Once, at *Pitchfork,* after interviewing the rapper Lil Yachty, he told me I looked like a *Seinfeld* character. "Jerry?" I asked, hopeful. Alas, no.) But in the absence of happiness, I sought easy pleasure. Shoving cookies down my throat nonstop was the solution at which I'd arrived. Feel bad, eat a cookie. I imagined life like the scales of justice. Grief weighed down one side, so I was within my rights to pour a mountain of Reese's Pieces on the other to achieve a counterbalance. But there was never enough candy to get the scales back to neutral. I know, because I tried.

I asked my therapist if she would be sad if I died because my veins were full of butter. She said she would be sad I was dead, but mostly she hoped if I went out that way, I would have made the decision to eat myself to death consciously. She had a point. I vowed to be aware of what I was feeding myself and no longer do it as a knee-jerk reaction to pain, devouring like a zombie. Sometimes it worked, sometimes it did not. One month, I quit sugar entirely. I couldn't trust myself to regulate, so I went cold turkey. I lost weight quickly. But I felt miserable. So I went back to sweets. An imperfect solution was still, by definition, a solution, and I did not really have any better ideas. I was putting a lot of effort into not thinking about Renzo, especially not thinking about the circumstances of his death. This was not a smart idea. The pressure was building up.

My hands and fingers began to hurt whenever I thought of him. It felt like my joints had a headache. I imagine this is what dogs feel when they bark at the sky before an oncoming storm.

In therapy one day I decided to talk about it. It did not go well. Toward the end of the session I began to narrate the night of his aneurysm. The firefighters, his pajamas. My hands started throbbing. I tried to continue, but I could not. I felt dizzy and confused. I am not usually at a loss for words, nor do I typically find myself unable to sit up straight. My therapist's office is on the basement level, down a semisteep set of stairs. Emerging onto the sidewalk when the session ended, I felt like I was coming up for air too quickly, like I had the bends. It was midmorning and I was in the West Village. I was supposed to go home and get back to work. I had a meeting. I couldn't imagine getting on the subway. I was pacing, dizzy. "Ask for what you need." What did I need? A hug. Where do you get a hug at 11:00 A.M. on a Wednesday in Manhattan?

I called my friend Jason (a different Jason from Jayson—no *Y*). A photographer about a decade older than me, Jason had a menagerie of tattoos, a mariner's beard, a booming voice, and a relentless drive to succeed. I admired him, felt like he was my older brother. He had a predilection for lovingly making fun of me that could occasionally work to deflate some of my self-seriousness. That was not what I was experiencing now, but I thought, *Close enough*. Jason also had a studio on Canal Street where I figured he'd be. I called him, and he confirmed that he was there and invited me to join him.

I decided to catch a cab and lurched toward Seventh Avenue. I felt drunk, frantic, as if the destabilizing that grief had done to my mind had finally leaked into my body. At the time, I was adhering to Covid guidelines around public transit, and when I reached into my pocket for my face mask, I found it was gone. Had I dropped it in the therapist's office? I doubled back, descended the stairs, and knocked on her window. "Do you have my mask?" I called through the window with some accusation. She let me back in and I checked the floor, pulled up the couch cushions. It had disappeared. This felt like an insurmountable problem. Then, with dawning glee, I realized I could get a new mask. But where? I hit the street and started peeking in storefronts. An upscale salon had a box of masks sitting on a shelf in the window.

The front door was locked, probably to keep out people like me. But I could see a man sitting at a reception desk in the middle of the room. I knocked on the door. I must have looked deranged. *Can I buy a mask?* I mouthed through the glass. I'd removed a dollar from my pocket and waved it at him as proof of concept. He opened the door and, with disgust, rejected my dollar, ordered me to take a mask and get lost. The door locked behind him. I hailed a yellow cab and headed to Chinatown.

Jason buzzed me in. His studio is on the third floor, and I hauled my body up the stairs. He met me at the door and gave me a bear hug. I turned my head to the side, put my ear to his chest, and cried and cried. He sat me on the couch to settle down. I tried to explain what had happened, how I'd tried to alleviate some of the pressure. I was overwhelmed, speaking in clipped nonsentences. I told him Allegra was pregnant. And then I asked him, "If this baby dies too, then do I get to kill myself?"

He laughed at me. "No!"

I don't know what I expected him to say. I don't know if my question was rhetorical or not, but his wholesale rejection of it as nonsense gave me what I needed. I snapped out of it.

My phone dinged. It was time for my meeting discussing the editorial team's upcoming stories with the advertising team. I dialed in on my phone and talked about our plans like everything was normal, and thus it was.

I was grateful for Jason's warmth. I was lucky to have a place to go when I needed one. But after this episode, I realized I didn't want to live emergency to emergency. My explosion that day was proof I had to face facts. It had happened. Renzo had died, and I needed help.

To confront that truth and unburden myself from even some of its weight, my therapist recommended I try a type of therapy called EMDR. EMDR, she explained, stands for "eye movement desensitization and reprocessing." It has been used routinely as treatment for PTSD, often with soldiers who've returned home from war. Not to be too dramatic about it, but EMDR is for people who, like me, have witnessed death.

According to Dr. Francine Shapiro, the originator of EMDR, the treatment can "be used to help support family members dealing with the death of a loved one," as she wrote in a medical journal. "The results of both prolonged debilitation and sudden death can involve trauma symptoms that include distressing intrusive images of the suffering patient. The family member is often unable to retrieve positive memories of the deceased, which further exacerbates and complicates the grieving process." That sounded a bit highfalutin, if largely spot on. I was hopeful my hands might stop hurting.

The way EMDR works is, basically, by doing the exact opposite of what I had been doing. Instead of dodging your most nightmarish memories altogether until they drip out of your subconscious and pile up until you inevitably succumb to their colossal scale, you ease into the memories, one scintilla at a time.

To do this, you take an initial fragment of the feared memory and narrate it slowly. When you begin to tense up, you pull back. You rub your legs, bounce your knees, cry, until you regain equilibrium. Then you start again. You go a little further into the memory, then a little further, and a little further, each time stopping along the way to gather yourself. Eventually, with retelling, the memory's power should lessen, the haunting diminish, the insurmountable becoming surmountable.

Also, you do all this while moving your eyes back and forth quickly, which somehow serves to rewire your brain. How? Unclear. Science hasn't totally yet figured out how EMDR works.

My therapist recommended a few potential practitioners, including a social worker named Sara, who specialized in this kind of therapy. She had the same name and job as my sister, which felt like a good omen. When we spoke on the phone, Sara was kind and patient. She expressed compassion without pandering. She didn't dismiss my pain or dwell on it. Pain was an ancient fact of life to be reckoned with. Like a dinosaur bone in your backyard, it's something that preexists you.

I liked Sara's website. Pale yellow with stock images of people basking in the sun's rays.

In our first meeting, Sara told me we'd actually be using a mix of EMDR and something called somatic experiencing. And then she told me a story about deer. Peter A. Levine, the originator of somatic experiencing, she said, had spent time observing animals in the wild. He noticed that deer, after escaping peril, like narrowly avoiding being hit by a car or a hunter's shot, would shake. They would, Levine says, "vibrate, twitch, and lightly tremble" to slough off the heightened emotion of the brush with danger.

"One of the difficulties in treating trauma has been the undue focus on the content of an event that has engendered trauma," Levine writes in his book *Waking the Tiger: Healing Trauma*. "Trauma sufferers tend to identify themselves as survivors, rather than as animals with an instinctual power to heal. The animal's ability to rebound from threat can serve as a model for humans. It gives us a direction that may point the way to our own innate healing abilities. We must pay attention to our animal nature to find the instinctive strategies needed to release us from trauma's debilitating effects."

As Sara was describing this all to me, I found myself anxiously tapping my knees. She said that was a good thing.

I was sitting in my living room, talking with her over Zoom. I'd stacked my laptop on top of a pile of books to raise it to my eyeline, to reduce slouching. Good posture felt important. Before we began talking about memories, Sara asked me to identify three objects in the room, which would serve to remind me that I was, in fact, in a room. I chose the Ornette Coleman poster hanging on the wall in a gold frame I'd gotten at an antique store in Connecticut, a small ceramic cat perched on the record shelf, and the Rubik's Cube beside it. They formed an isosceles triangle of reality. Sara instructed me to feel my feet on the floor. I pressed my toes into the ground. I was not wearing any socks.

Sara continued. Though the "EM" in EMDR stands for "eye movement," she said, many people practice the therapy with any number of varieties of repetitive motion. She preferred an audio method and emailed me a link to a very spare website with a small Play button and a drop-down menu with which to select different sounds, various dings and bloops. I inherently trusted the site's rudimentary design; if it hadn't needed updating in years, hopefully there was a good reason. I chose the "thud" sound, which had a vaguely wet feel to it. I put on my headphones and the thud panned from my left ear to my right, back and forth.

Sara asked me to imagine a place where I felt safe. Before talking about Renzo's death, we were going to practice reprocessing by using a good memory instead of a bad one. I thought about a vacation Allegra and I had taken years earlier, as a newish couple, to the Rockhouse, a hotel in Jamaica that got its name from the craggy cliffs at the edge of the property that dropped off into the sea. There were ladders drilled into the rock faces, and you could descend right into the turquoise water. We spent the week eating, reading, and swimming in the Caribbean. One day, we took a boat ride to a reef to snorkel. I couldn't see the fish too well without my glasses. It didn't matter. Mostly, we were sedentary.

I loved being with Allegra like this. Removed from the world of work and stress, before Covid, before Renzo, it was the most serene our life had ever been. Her happiness was my happiness. For years, the background photo of my phone was a picture of her walking down Rockhouse's tiled path to the water, a blue mat for floating in the ocean curled up under her arm. I changed it only after Renzo was born.

"What color was the ladder into the ocean?" Sara asked. Red, I said. "Red," she said. "Tell me what else you see."

I described our vacation in increasingly vivid detail. I'd speak, and Sara would repeat what I said. We continued this process for the rest of the session.

Sara and I met twice a week. With my feet solidly on the floor, my headphones on, and the thud going from ear to ear, I began to revisit the night it happened. I'd describe the brief moments between when Renzo cried out and when we called 911, when the reality of his condition was not yet clear. How Allegra and I, as we tried to wake him, put a bag of frozen vegetables on his body to attempt to shock him into consciousness, how the seriousness of what was occurring began to creep into view, like a heavy velvet curtain very slowly coming down at the end of an act.

I didn't even know if I should call 911. "This might be ridiculous," I'd said to the operator, and now repeated to Sara. "I just want to be on the safe side."

In the living room, on Zoom, my body shook. Like the deer. I wept. I wailed. Sara had me pause. Through the door, I heard Allegra turn up the volume on the stereo in the other room. She was blasting talk radio to drown me out.

Sara and I repeated this process for several weeks, about ninety minutes at a time, attacking a small portion of the pain, animating its source, pausing to expunge its physicality. Eventually, my hands and fingers stopped aching. It was a miracle. Or science. Some combination of the two.

I'd made it beyond an impasse. The brick wall that I had been smashing my head into had begun to crumble. What lay on its other side?

I began to be able to remember Renzo without absolute distress. The treatment had not taken away the basic fact of his death. That would always be true. Sadness would remain constant. But not terror. A low bar to clear, but a clearance nonetheless. The boy who was my son, who was alive, but who now is not, began to reemerge in my mind, which is, I would need to accept, where he lived now. Thinking of him was bittersweet, but not always with the emphasis on the bitter.

My grief was unique, as is everyone's, and maybe Renzo's death was a rare type of loss, but for most people, grief's essence, whatever its cause, can be boiled down to an emptiness that needs to be filled. "Grief needs to be witnessed," says David Kessler, imploring you not to go it alone. Implied in that directive is something it took some time for me to understand: that I actually needed to grieve in the first place. Grief is an act, not a state of being. A verb, not a noun. You need to experience the pain, not run from it. The work I did with Sara showed me that maybe my wounds were not so deep, but in avoiding them, I'd let them fester.

I had wanted to die after Renzo's death, a desire that felt justified. But I had chosen not to. I had continued living, and I'd now need to make peace with that decision.

Renzo's life had given me purpose. This was selfish, but having a child is selfish. You pretend it is the opposite, that you're giving life, that you're nurturing it, that you're participating in the future. But parenthood is for the parents. I wanted to be a father to placate gnawing boredom and narcissism's latent tug. I wanted to nurture someone who looked like me, to feel pride for a child where perhaps I felt none for myself. I wanted to watch this child grow and succeed, and to let that fill me with feeling. That was no longer possible. I hoped I might one day live a life of redeeming value, but simply realizing there was going to be a "one day" felt like enough for now. My immediate challenge remained filling the time.

The first thing I needed to do, as Allegra urged, was care for myself. I'd always been attuned to that mentally, but I had more of an adversarial relationship with my physical care. After a dutiful month of *Yoga with Adriene,* I dropped off exercise. Mainlining snickerdoodles was not a long-term nutrition plan. When was the last time I'd had a physical? Allegra asked me. I didn't even have a primary care doctor.

She helped me find one and I reluctantly made an appointment. The doctor was nice enough, though she seemed somewhat bewildered by my disclosure that I did not have a colon. As we talked, I sat beside her desk while she took notes on a computer. I glanced at the screen and saw that she was googling "colitis."

Aside from that, the exam was relatively normal, as was I. She noted my weight and suggested I make what she called "lifestyle changes." I did have one thing on my mind I was nervous about, and before I left, I worked up the courage to ask her about it.

A saggy paunch had developed in my right armpit. It dangled like a cat's belly, a soft half-moon. I was scared it was cancer, or somehow something worse. The doctor gave it a poke. "I'm not sure what that is," she said, which was not reassuring. She told me I needed a scan. I made an appointment for a few weeks later at a small hospital in Manhattan.

When I arrived that morning, I told them my name at the front desk and the receptionist directed me to the mammogram department. "This is for my armpit," I said. She repeated her instructions and sent me on my way.

In the office, they assured me I was in the right place.

"This is for my armpit," I said again, slightly bewildered. They told me to take a seat. I filled out an intake form on an iPad and waited anxiously. Forty-five minutes later, I went back to the desk to ask if I would be seen soon. They looked at me quizzically. My appointment wasn't for another fifteen minutes. I'd arrived an hour early.

When I was eventually shown into an exam room, it was clear that I would, in fact, be having a mammogram. A cheerful technician ordered me to remove my shirt and placed stickers on my nipples. She told me she often gave mammograms to men, who often got cancer in their breast tissue. Then she squeezed my chest between two plates of glass. She did the same on my normal armpit, the left one, and then the bulbous right one. She took images and examined them on a monitor. Things were inconclusive, she said, and I was excused back to the waiting room.

I started to spiral. Of course I would have male breast cancer. It made perfect sense. Nothing good had ever happened to me, nothing good would ever happen to me. Renzo's death was not a turning point but an end point. I was stupid to have imagined I'd ever learn anything from it other than absolute nihilism.

The technician called my name and showed me into a new exam room. I'd need to have an ultrasound. She ordered me to remove my shirt again, lie down, and raise my right arm over my head. She squirted my armpit with the blue gel I'd seen the obstetricians smear over Allegra's pregnant stomach dozens of times. It was cold. I was freaking out.

She rubbed the ultrasound wand on my armpit, and a

black-and-white image of it appeared on a monitor. After a moment, she excused herself to confer with a doctor. Before she left, she gave me a handful of brown paper towels to wipe myself up. I was just putting my shirt back on when she returned. After a quick conference, they'd determined everything was fine. The protuberance in my armpit was an accumulation of fat. An unusual place for it to congregate, but benign in all senses. They sent me and my lump back home.

That night, I went out for a drink with my friend to celebrate my newfound health. We walked to a bar in the neighborhood, and as soon as we got there, we saw a woman I knew having a drink with her friend. I'd not spoken to her about Renzo, which was normal, as we were not too close. But she knew. Upon seeing me, she began to blurt out condolences. She was pretty drunk and rambling. I had absolutely no interest in having this conversation. I already knew Renzo had died and that it was terrible. I wanted to talk to my friend about something else. Anything else. I wanted to be normal.

While I dealt with that, my friend began talking to the woman's friend. They quickly started bantering. I was listening with one ear when I heard the guy raise his voice in excitement.

"So did you pee on him?!"

"I peed on him!"

They'd fallen through a vortex into a spicy world of chitchat while I was being further punished for Renzo's death. I got the pee context later (an experimental music performance / sex party they'd coincidentally both attended), though for a while I was stuck being consoled by a drunk. It was what she needed, not me. I don't think this woman did anything wrong. If I saw someone I knew whose child had died, I would also express my sorrow. I hope it would not be unwanted. I hope I'd be sober. But if I was making their life worse, would I know? I didn't say anything to her as she spoke; I just stood there and listened. That was my new lot in life. The day's path may not have ended in cancer, but it would not end in pee.

The summer was a nothing period. We were waiting for the baby, who was not coming soon. Work kept me busy, which was a virtue. But Vice was tiptoeing toward bankruptcy. All the employees felt a tenuous connection to the day-to-day as we awaited the inevitable crash. That collective panic infused a not unwelcome bit of camaraderie, if not much in the way of fulfillment. For that, I would need to look elsewhere.

For Allegra, returning to work after Renzo's death had provided purpose and thus relief. She was a savvy employee, an attuned navigator of an office environment's subtle mechanics of power. Work was a game with its own rules, ones I often seemed blind to but that Allegra understood innately. She's good with systems, satisfied with the completion of an assignment. She can watch a YouTube video on how to do some complex, technical task and mimic it without difficulty. She was able, for example, to handily disassemble the stereo in my Volvo to install an off-brand aux cord, a multistep process that necessitated use of a mini screwdriver. With a gun to my head, I could never. Allegra has said she doesn't have a big imagination, and maybe that's true, and maybe that is why she is so tied to order, but her curiosity, her openness to the world, is something I have always loved about her. Renzo's death wore away some of that. There's less safety in the unexplored than in the known.

Early on in our relationship, Allegra took me to see an exhibit of paintings by Giorgio Morandi. The paintings were muted still lifes of ceramics. She spent time studying each small canvas, quietly absorbing the bowls and vases. I liked them fine, but I loved seeing her so enraptured.

Soon after, she began watching videos of expert potters on the wheel, centering their clay with great focus. It made sense she was drawn to it, a methodical way to be creative. For a birthday gift, I bought her a semester of pottery classes at a studio in Manhattan. She took to it. I loved watching her leave for class, heading to the subway in leggings and an oversize T-shirt, and return later, the same clothes streaked with clay.

When she returned to pottery class after Renzo's death, she found that her love of the work had not waned. By then, she had been studying for several years and had become quite skilled. She produced elegant, unfussy pieces. She'd refined her technique over time, the edges of her jars sharper, the curves of her vases more supple. Her glazes were always simple, a midnight blue, a speckled white, or a mossy green, sometimes with a diagonal stripe bisecting two colors, but never more.

To become an accomplished ceramicist making pottery on the wheel, as she did, requires a unique combination of imagination and control. From a hunk of clay to a flowerpot is both a messy and a mathematical journey, right and left brains working in congress. I imagined her at the wheel, in extreme, liberating concentration. It suited her. When I suggested from time to time that she try to sell some of her pots, she always dismissed the idea. This was not a business but a hobby. Her work lined our shelves at home. If a visitor admired a piece, she gave it to them.

I wanted that, to become besotted and productive like Allegra. But I wasn't sure what to indulge in. I was focused on finding something that would eat time, which is not a particularly good approach to discovering a new passion. Instead of using my free time to organically explore any nascent interests, I mostly puttered. It was like every day I was spending so long trying to decide what movie to watch that I ran out of time to actually watch one.

One friend suggested a trip to the thrift store one Saturday afternoon. We drove to the Hempstead Salvation Army store on Long Island, about forty-five minutes away. The store was enormous. Looking through every rack, shirt by shirt, ate time, a lot of it. I didn't find much, though, a white Brooks Brothers button-down shirt, which I thought would be useful to have, and a T-shirt with a drawing of two yellow Labs in a rowboat that said "the dog days of summer." Stopping at a second shop in Queens on the way back home, I found a long-sleeve black T-shirt from the skateboarding brand Spitfire. It featured the brand's mascot, a character named Flameboy, an animated, smiling ball of fire. The shirt was from the nineties and I thought it was so cool, but it was a medium, too small for me. It was only a few bucks, though, and I couldn't just leave it there. Maybe, I thought, I could sell it. A few days later, I listed it on eBay. I took photos of the shirt's front and back, its tag, a close-up of the graphic, another of the minuscule copyright line. I took measurements of the sleeves from the shoulder to the cuff, its length from the collar to the hem, its width from left armpit to right, and wrote a description of its overall condition. In decent shape, no flaws.

The auction got several bids, and I sold the shirt for sixty dollars, about ten times what I paid for it. I was proud of myself. It wasn't that I needed the money but that I was able to earn it by seeing something in the shirt that others had not. If one man's trash was another man's treasure, I took pleasure in being their middleman. The whole process was time-consuming and tedious, and gave me a small hit of dopamine. It dawned on me that this might be the type of hobby I was searching for.

When I was a child, my parents dragged my sister and me to antique stores, where we moped down the aisles, miserable, as they dug through piles of rusty tin signs and beach pails. Of course, in my own way, I'd become them. I started spending every Saturday driving out of the city to thrift shops, flea markets, estate sales. This was why my pull to celebrate the discovery of rare records during the shivah was so magnetic. It was the satisfaction of an innate impulse, one most ancient and Jewish: the finding of a deal.

So I began spending Saturdays searching for clothes to resell, driving to small towns in New Jersey and Long Island, accumulating hundreds of garments. I sorted the inventory into large clear plastic bins. Allegra made me labels. I started with men's clothes and slowly expanded into women's. For each item I listed for sale, I would go through the process:

wash, dry, steam, photograph, measure, describe, post. Everything sold needed to be packaged, measured, weighed, and dropped at the post office. I don't know if, in Kessler's definition, selling used clothing on the internet counts as meaning, but like the expectation of reciting the kaddish every day, its benefit was in its ritual. The haphazard does not ascribe purpose like the routine.

Each evening after work I would list items for sale, usually beside Allegra in bed as we watched TV. I liked simultaneously being near her and being busy. I felt less needy. As I gained success selling, I decided to move off eBay to an app called Depop. It served a similar marketplace function as eBay, but it was specific to clothing. I padded out my profile. I offered plain, unpretentious staples. Timeless clothing, mostly cotton, a lot of faded blue. I had a fondness for shirts with illustrations of dogs or other animals. Anything weathered. I settled on a tagline ("Vintage basics and fun surprises") and, eventually, a store name, "Schnip's Picks." A garden to tend.

I had to try hard not to be too cloying as I fawned over the clothes in the descriptions. "A perfect vintage Jerzees black raglan sleeve crewneck," I wrote. "Ultimate staple. Lots of wear on this. No flaws. Well loved." What I wanted to say is that your life would be changed if you just forked over twenty dollars to me and I sent you a sweatshirt. That is how I felt. I loved these clothes. I *believed* in them. These were my babies; I wanted them to go to a good home. Depop is popular largely with people in their teens and twenties without a lot of money to spend, and my switch from eBay was not a sound business decision, but I was dedicated to the idea that whoever was purchasing beat-up jean shorts from me was also buying into the idea of me. It honestly made me feel less alone.

Occasionally, while shopping for things to sell, I would find something I loved that would send me down a rabbit hole. I stumbled onto a T-shirt with a bunch of cows playing basketball. It was so cute, so odd. There was a signature at the bottom of the illustration: Woody Jackson. Researching him, I found he was best known for painting the iconic cow logo of Ben & Jerry's ice cream. In the eighties and nineties, he'd capitalized on that cow's ubiquity with a clothing line of cow shirts. There were basketball cows, golf cows, hockey cows, skiing cows, cows in a marching band, cows at a square dance. Then there were the cow parodies: Chairman Mao became Chairman Moo. There was a cow/kangaroo hybrid, the kangamoo, a cow-print convertible, the Cowdil-lac. There were a handful of straightforward non-cow shirts—a trio of German shepherds, a slice of cherry pie—but it was pretty much all just cows.

I started to read about Jackson and found he had a master's degree in painting from Yale. He clearly could have branched out from bovines. I admired and envied that he did not. What makes a man have such a singular vision? What would it be like to know what you wanted? To know what made you feel good and pursue it? So what if it was cows?

I was pursuing selling clothing steadily, at least. But sales were slow. Then one day I woke up to dozens of orders. What had happened? A friend emailed me: I'd been featured in a popular email newsletter about fashion. They said my

Depop offerings were "casually advanced." Each item they highlighted (including a yellow canvas bag lined with little frogs that had been languishing) sold. It took me hours to retrieve, pack, and ship all the orders. Mindless bliss. Or, at the very least, not pain.

I wrote a thank-you note to the newsletter's writer and offered to send him a piece of clothing as a gesture of thanks. I also explained why I had started selling clothes, that my son had died and I needed to avoid thinking about him by occupying my time with tedium. I felt compelled to tell him. Unable not to, as though in writing about me without the mention of Renzo, he'd told an incomplete story. He sent his condolences. In the name of journalistic integrity, though, he said he'd have to turn down the gift.

After some shake-ups at work, I got a new boss, an often-difficult-to-reach guy who lived in the Catskills. He was sharp and charming, but his attention to detail was low. In our weekly meetings, when they happened, I struggled with the generality of his directives. But he was kind to me. When Renzo died, he'd mailed me a bunch of soup.

Where we did connect was talking about old clothes, thrift stores, and estate sales. He was from the Southwest originally, and his mom would pick up turquoise jewelry for him, which he would resell at a markup in the Northeast. He turned me on to the website AuctionZip, a platform for auction houses big and small. The big was not new—the site's listings for expensive art and antiques were the same as those on other major auction sites. But the small stuff was fun to browse. Need a leaf blower and a shotgun from some guy's garage in Iowa? They've got you covered.

As my online selling started eating up more time, I started to fantasize about having a storefront. In addition to clothes, I'd sell magazines, records, cassettes, books. The stuff of life. Sometimes, if I picked up something extra special at an estate sale or a thrift store, I wouldn't list it for sale immediately, imagining that I was holding back the best goods for the grand opening of my store. Did I actually believe that? No, I didn't. The economic upside to opening your own knickknack shop is not high, especially in New York City, where rent is catastrophic. I was making hundreds of dollars a month on Depop, not a negligible amount of money but nothing close to proof of concept. I had no actual intention to quit my job, rent a space, and start selling clothes. But the fantasy was nice when most things were not.

On AuctionZip I came across an auction listing for a box of old motorcycle magazines. I don't know anything about motorcycles and, honestly, I think they are very dangerous, but they do look cool. The magazines were from the fifties, sixties, and seventies, featuring an array of sleek, retro looks I thought might be good for people's coffee tables. I put in a lowball bid and, uncontested, won. A week later, a forty-pound box of magazines, catalogs, and repair manuals arrived via FedEx. Allegra could not have rolled her eyes back in her head any farther. "I thought the box would be bigger," she said. I tried to sell them cheaply at a stoop sale and even ventured back to eBay, but I'd misjudged. No one wanted them.

What do you do with forty pounds of motorcycle magazines? Around the corner from my therapist's office is a bookstore that stocks old magazines. On their website, they say they do buy used items but encourage you to email photos of what you have for sale before walking in unannounced. I composed a note, taking pains to be nonchalant and agreeable.

> Love your shop and thought this might be something you'd be interested in? I've got about 100 50s/60s/70s motorcycle magazines. Mostly *Cycle World,* and then some random stuff like catalogs. Some pictures attached. Everything in good shape, some better than others but no major issues. Let me know what you think:) open to selling all or a few or even trading. Thanks so much for considering!

The shop owner responded that he would be open to making a "judicious selection." I packed them into a large camo backpack I'd picked up at a yard sale and, after a therapy appointment, walked over.

I introduced myself as the motorcycle magazine guy and unpacked my bag. I'd also brought a few other books I'd found recently, including a first edition of *The Counterlife* by Philip Roth. His favorite Roth, he said warmly. I felt proud of myself. He and his business partner flipped through the magazines while I browsed the shelves. I looked at a William Wegman picture book for children. Like Woody Jackson, Wegman was a man of singular zoological vision, though with dogs in place of cows. Specifically Weimaraners, the large, short-haired gray-brown breed of which he is enamored and that he dressed up in human clothes and posed in fairy-tale vignettes and other scenes. The book, a hardcover edition of Wegman's *ABC,* featured photos of docile dogs arranged in all twenty-six letters of the alphabet. I thought I'd bring it home for the new baby.

The shop owner made me an offer for a selection of the magazines, which I happily agreed to. And then I started talking, spewing words at him. I could not help myself. I told him about Renzo. I explained, in detail, about how, after you have a child and then that child dies, time doesn't change, but how you use it so drastically does. That you need to find ways to fill the day, and for me that meant a forty-pound box of motorcycle magazines.

He froze up. Sensing I'd gone too far, I backtracked, tried to be normal. I work at a cool website, I told him; we should have our social media team do a video about the store. Never mind that that's not really what we did, nor did I have editorial oversight of social media. Sure, he said, that would be great. I said I'd be in touch. He handed me a check, and I packed up the remaining magazines and the Wegman book and went back home.

With hindsight, I can see that selling things was not a hobby. It had hobby-like elements, but it was not an escape. Filling your time with tasks is not the same as healing your pain; it's something you do to avoid it. What I'd unknowingly done was give myself a new job, the thing I'd historically used to measure my worth. I'd unconsciously re-created the structure of power I resented. Every teenage Depop shopper was my boss. I felt good when I had a sale, bad when I didn't, neither of which I could control. I'd again farmed out my feelings, my potential peace, to others. My bottomless need for reassurance was a problem that existed long before Renzo and that the isolation his death begat had exacerbated. Much later, I'd learn that what I needed to do was not fill the hole but address why it was empty in the first place.

Even now, though, I still sell clothes. I can't quite help myself. I don't make it out to Long Island or New Jersey as much, but I stop at every stoop sale I come across. Not so long ago, after seeing a paisley pattern at the top of a garbage can, I found myself digging through a bag of trash and brought home an overflowing armload of clothes, which, over the course of several hours, I washed, steamed, photographed, measured, and listed for sale.

I decided to revisit the Henry Rollins interview idea and pitch it to another publication, one he might find acceptable. I still felt like he could tell me what to do, as he always had, that he held the key to whatever door I needed to walk through. Through a friend, I got in touch with a magazine editor and sent him my idea. After some back-and-forth, he said he'd discussed the story with his colleagues. Sometime later, he called me with his response. "We're worried about you," he said. That was not something I'd expected. At first I was angry. I felt like I wasn't being taken seriously. Then I was humbled, and touched. And then I changed my pitch.

What does grief sound like? I proposed an essay that would ask that question. Renzo's cry, EMDR, Dua Lipa, Bill

Callahan, Black Flag, Allegra's voice on speakerphone as I drove home from the thrift store. To someone else grieving, to someone else in pain, the through line of their experience could be basketball, baking, skincare, books, video games. Looking at the sound of grief was a way of making the intangible tangible. It was a specific if arbitrary way of looking for patterns when there are none, making up constellations in a vast and dark sky.

Though they declined to have me interview Rollins, after some back-and-forth, the magazine accepted my essay pitch. Though I pride myself on hitting deadlines, I was incredibly late turning in a draft. It took me months to write the essay because I didn't have any idea what I wanted to say. But it was helpful to say it anyway; grief must be witnessed. I ultimately didn't write much about Rollins, but I spent a while talking about the R&B singer Frank Ocean.

Ocean may be a singer, but saying he's just a singer is like saying Galileo was just a stargazer. Technically accurate, spiritually insufficient. What his music, sprawling and impressionistic, has managed to do is to boil down the experience of being human, its beauty and futility, the quintessential journey to know ourselves and others, to experience, to feel connection, curiosity, and satiation. I'd say I was overreaching, but he's inspired a fandom of frenzied adoration that makes my slobbering praise look faint at best.

I used to listen to Ocean's album *Blonde* constantly before Renzo died. After, it was too much. One big feeling at a time. Months went by after his death before I gave it a shot again, in the Volvo, during a light snowfall, with my beloved friend Alex and Allegra both asleep as I ferried them back to the city from a weekend away at a friend's cabin. Ocean can write a straightforward song, but I preferred his more obtuse gestures. His lyrics can be corny or they can be beautiful, oftentimes both. About love: "When you're not here, I'll save some for you." The distillation of every act of kindness in the history of time in nine words. He's not Ovid, but only because we don't live in ancient Rome. "Solo" is my favorite song on the album. After months of so much music sounding distorted and harrowing, it felt almost disorientingly familiar. I sang along quietly, so as not to wake them. "Forgot to tell you / Gotta tell you how much I vibe with you / And we don't gotta be solo." The song is about romantic love, but it doesn't havc to be.

I loved the moments on the album when Ocean hands the microphone to his friends, seemingly with no idea or concern what they'll say. It's like he just wanted to hear their voices. One "song" didn't include Ocean at all, only audio of a Frenchman lamenting his girlfriend breaking up with him because he wouldn't add her on Facebook. *Blonde* ends with a nine-minute song that's Ocean and a group of his friends talking. "How far is a light-year?" one of them asks. "One second" is the response. Then the album ends.

There is a real answer to the light-year question, though it's not phrased quite right. A light-year isn't a measurement of distance but of distance traveled. The answer is that over 365 days, light will journey approximately 5.88 trillion miles. But that's not my answer. How far is a light-year? *Very far,* I would say, *but Renzo, you're right here next to me.*

Though we never really considered giving Renzo the name Frank Ocean Schnipper, it was discussed. Sitting in a diner, months before he was born, we were spitballing names. Henry Rollins Schnipper, I said. A joke; I knew that was not going to fly. Frank Ocean Schnipper. Allegra and I both loved Frank, dreamy musician with power and softness in equal amounts. An ideal way to be for our boy. But maybe that was too wholesale a theft, not quite a tribute. Besides, Frank Ocean wasn't even his real name. It's Christopher Breaux. And he usually went by Lonny. We couldn't steal his chosen name. If our child wanted to change his name later, so be it. But let him start with a clean slate.

Allegra had a list of Italian names. If she could get one of those over the line, she said, I could have free rein on the middle name. It was a tempting offer. In the diner, she read them off. Luca. Roman. Renzo. Like the architect Renzo Piano. I liked that. The *Z* was fun. Renzo Rollins, I said. The double *R* sounded good. Renzo Rollins Schnipper. About as stupid as it comes. A dumb idea we'd never actually go for. Unless.

As summer waned, I hoped to get out more. I wanted to enjoy my time, not just kill it. I'd been lonely, with a chip on my shoulder about the solitary onus of grief. This became something of a self-fulfilling prophecy, with a presumption of isolation begetting actual isolation. I waffled between wanting to feel normal and feeling deep in my bones that I was not normal, would never again be normal. These two parts were typically not in harmony. The former wanted to hang out with friends, go see a concert, do what I used to do, and be who I used to be. The latter wanted to seethe. Seething was, unfortunately, easier. I fought against it, but I didn't always win.

One night, when an old friend moved into a new place and asked me to come see it, I accepted the invitation. He said he'd gotten tie-dyed beanbag chairs. I wanted to see. I'd been saying no to social invitations unless they were maximally convenient for me, like in my living room, where I didn't have to stand up or pay attention. But I wanted to be the kind of friend who pays a housewarming visit. It sounded nice in theory, but I was not ready. As the night approached and I was weighed down with grief, it became clear I wasn't going to leave the couch. I explained to him over text how I was feeling, and I canceled. I felt bad—I didn't want to be a flake—but I also felt that my grief allowed me a perennial trump card. He understood.

Scrolling through my phone, I saw on Instagram that, a quick walk from my apartment, a musician I liked was performing a small show at a bar. I thought that might be a low-pressure distraction. Would he want to meet me there instead? I texted him to ask.

"I do not," he responded. "Feeling peaceful. Have fun."

I was incensed. Peaceful? How could I explain to someone that I needed them to get on the subway, give up 5 percent of their peace, and tithe it to me? How could I explain that I would never feel peace? I didn't even try. Instead I sat there, staring into space, buzzing with rage. I didn't want to be, but I couldn't help it. I was so angry. I was so sad. The latter was fueling the former through a process of weird osmosis. I hated it.

Throughout my life, I'd never gotten comfortable with anger. I bristled at it in others, viewed it as impatience, misdirected frustration. If I was the angry one, I felt physically repulsed by the heat that grew inside me. When I avoided it for too long, I would explode, which would not offer relief, only shame. My relationship with anger got more complicated after Renzo's death. One of Kübler-Ross's stages of grief is anger. So was I allowed some of it? And where would I direct it? At a peaceful friend seemed like the wrong place, but I didn't really understand what other options I had.

It was easier for me to be generous with strangers than with friends, with those on the outskirts of my life than with those in my inner circle. I expected, fairly or not, that, based on how close with someone I was before Renzo died, I'd receive a corresponding amount of attention from them after. But things don't work that way. In the face of tragedy, not everyone shines. I'm including myself in that equation, too.

Allegra encouraged me to get out of the house that night, and in some attempt to spite both my friend and myself, I went to the concert alone, sulking. I walked the three blocks to the venue and sat down at the bar and ordered a Coke. A man in the crowd caught my eye, and I thought I recognized him because he was an actor, but then he approached me and said hi. I'd recognized him because I knew him, but my brain was too decrepit to properly place him. He was a guy I knew from the music industry. We made small talk about his job calculating royalty payments for musicians. He didn't mention Renzo. I don't know if he knew he'd died. I don't know if he knew he even existed in the first place. I was grateful for that brief visit to another world. It was the best part of the night. Fittingly for my bad mood, the concert was not good. I had trouble telling the difference between the sound check and the performance.

I look at that night now and wince. My friend didn't do anything wrong. I was the one who had flaked. I could have granted him even the smallest bit of latitude. Upholding the Golden Rule should not be dependent on reciprocity. I had wanted the night to lift me out of the doldrums, not confirm that I still lived there. Per Toni Morrison, I had been taking in heavy doses of beauty, but listening to piano music at home was too safe. I wanted beauty to give me a heart attack.

Around that time, I often found myself thinking of the opening scene of Paolo Sorrentino's movie *The Great Beauty,* where an Asian tourist is visiting Italy, admiring a fountain. The water is an icy blue, the marble a buttery tan. He leaves his tour group and walks to a ledge to take a photo of the expanse of the city. In the background, a heavenly-sounding vocal group is practicing choral music on a perch above the fountain. The tourist gazes in awe. He wipes his brow, then faints. *This,* I remember thinking, *this is what I need.*

There is a name for this experience, a syndrome characterized by a feeling of great overwhelm in the face of divine art. In his autobiography, diagnosing himself, the nineteenth-century French writer Marie-Henri Beyle, better known by his pen name, Stendhal, writes of the lightheadedness he felt simply being in Italy. "I was already in a kind of ecstasy by the idea of being in Florence, and the proximity of the great men whose tombs I had just seen. Absorbed in contemplating sublime beauty, I saw it close-up—I touched it, so to speak. I had reached that point of emotion where the heavenly sensations of the fine arts meet passionate feeling. As I emerged from Santa Croce, I had palpitations (what they call an attack of the nerves in Berlin); the life went out of me, and I walked in fear of falling."

In 1989, a Florentine psychiatrist began tracking patients who were admitted to the hospital with similar symptoms. Precipitating factors were, she wrote, "an impressionable personality, the stress of travel and the encounter with a city like Florence haunted by ghosts of the great, death and the perspective of history." She dubbed the condition Stendhal syndrome. To reverse the symptoms, she sent sufferers back home to their gray, artless lives.

I went to Florence once. As moving as the architecture of the city and the paintings in the Uffizi were, the city felt like too much of a tourist trap. Stendahl's ghost escaped me. Was his syndrome specific to European art? Or could you flutter from seeing a fountain locally? Did it even have to be about visual art at all? Might this feeling, this overwhelm, be what I'd felt so many times before while listening to music? Could Stendahl syndrome be what I felt listening to Frank Ocean in the car? To Black Flag as a boy? Perhaps not. Stendhal seemed like he was having a pretty good time, whereas my moments of musical revelation were mostly about transforming pain into something manageable.

I worried that was too unambitious a desire. I could do better. Listening to music had helped me hobble through my childhood illness, but Renzo's death was something else altogether. Should I not be aiming for wholesale spiritual realignment? Or was this not the time to be ambitious? I was caught in a worrying spiral. Days would be attuned not to the greater yearning you can do with an untroubled life but to the minutiae of the moment. I was paying close attention to what could potentially cause relief from pain, to make use of what had potential for transcendence and catalog what did not as I built new roads toward an unknown destination.

But even Stendhal was reliant on others. I didn't build fountains or write songs.

A few weeks later, I tried going to another concert, this time purposefully alone. Another person would only make things more complicated. A bummer of a realization but a realization nonetheless. The room was filled with cool people in their twenties who, before the performance, milled about, drinking beers, hugging one another, chatting casually. I was alone, drinking a seltzer, leaning against a wall, watching. Suddenly, some evil light switch flicked on inside me and I hated all of them. I hated their innocence and naïveté, their luck and privilege, their absolute ignorance of the calamities of life. As I watched the musicians, two singers gently harmonizing behind a conference table, heat rose in my chest. As soon as the performance ended, I rushed out of the venue.

I knew I couldn't go home, knew I couldn't talk to anyone. I needed to chill out. I took a walk and ended up at a record store, where I flipped through albums for an hour before panic buying an expensive LP by a band I didn't like because it was a good deal for a rare record.

I hated this resentment, resented it. But it felt inescapable, knee-jerk. It was not anyone's fault Renzo died. It was not anyone's fault I was in pain, not their fault they were not. I knew that intellectually, but emotionally not so much. Until my heart caught up with my head, I figured it was okay if I didn't want to be around people for a while. For a few months, I didn't go to concerts. A small concession, but in a desert of pleasure it felt like a significant sacrifice.

Then tickets went on sale for a performance by La Monte Young at Dream House. I'd never been and had always wanted to go, so I bought one. Originally conceived in the mid-1960s, Dream House is a sound and light installation that Young ran with his wife, Marian Zazeela (Zazeela died in 2024). Its latest manifestation, situated in a carpeted loft in Tribeca, has been around since 1993. Both Young and Zazeela are recognized as pioneers of musical minimalism, though they are less known than other avant-garde composers like Steve Reich or Philip Glass. Young is a pianist, and his six-hour piece for the instrument, "The Well-Tuned Piano," is a massive statement of restraint. I blew a bunch of money on eBay on a boxed set of the piece. Once, when I put it on at home, Allegra thought it was street noise.

Young is in his eighties and in poor health, and I'd never seen him perform, so I was glad I'd have the chance. The piece being performed was "Birthday Blues," from 1960, in honor of his and Zazeela's sixtieth wedding anniversary. "Birthday Blues" is an ensemble piece, and Young would be performing vocals, while Zazeela would be responsible for a lighting installation. My friend Amber said she wanted to come. She has a gentle air about her, and I was happy I'd be in her company. Before the performance, we caught up and ate turkey burgers at a nearby restaurant. The waitress was memorably nice and we talked for too long, so we arrived at Dream House at the last minute. Everyone's shoes were piled by the front door.

The room had already filled up, so we sat on the floor by the entryway. The main room is situated off a small hallway, and from our vantage point, to the left of the tabla player, we could only see the ensemble at an angle. Young was seated in a wheelchair, in the middle of his group's semicircle and only partially visible to us. With a scraggly white beard, dressed in his typical leather gear, he looked like the elder leader of a motorcycle gang. Zazeela, also in a wheelchair, was off to the side, an observer. I noticed she had dogs on her socks, which I thought was cute.

The music began. Young and his longtime disciple Jung Hee Choi harmonized a wordless chant. Slowly, the other instruments, guitar, bass, trumpet, and tabla, all entered. The music swelled. For about an hour, the musicians surfed along a groove. The room, lit in low purple, hummed. It was hot, but the cool air from the air conditioner, mounted on the wall by the doorway, hit Amber and me on the head first before traveling along to the rest of the attendees. We were comfortable. It was a great night. The music was entrancing, ancient. I felt overwhelmed, renewed, alive.

Young and his ensemble were performing "Birthday Blues" again the next night. I wanted to go back and get a good seat, to see Young unobscured. Tickets were sold out, but I emailed the Dream House and begged them to sell me one. They agreed.

I arrived early, before the doors opened, and waited in line. I was one of the first people inside and scored a spot on the floor a few feet from the ensemble. The room filled and the piece began. Sort of. Choi began to chant, but Young was clearly uncomfortable. The room was sweltering. The air-conditioning was outmatched. "Fan!" he yelled out into the room. Choi, still performing, picked up her phone and texted what I assume was a Dream House worker, who slunk out in front of the crowd and turned up the power on the small fan sitting beside Young. It was not enough. Young, displeased, writhed. "Fan!"

Eventually, a larger box fan was trotted out and set up

directly in front of Young. He was sweating profusely. He's a big man, and I worried his heart was going to stop. Was he going to die, right then, in front of me? Stranger things had happened. His band, clearly unnerved, hobbled through the piece. Maybe they shouldn't have. The performance was not good. When it ended, as people filed out, Young sat in the room, motionless, absorbing the fan's meager gusts. Should I not have gone back for a second night? I'd pushed my luck, and I was not a lucky man.

Allegra put less pressure on herself. I marveled at her ability to find satisfaction, enrichment, and distraction where I found only longing. What I mean is that she was perfectly happy to shut out the dumb outside world and just zone out and watch TV. She had become a massive Formula 1 racing fan after watching the Netflix documentary series *Drive to Survive*. The sport, wildly popular internationally, found a new audience in the U.S. with the series, which followed the individual teams, their drivers and coaches, across the racing season. While Lewis Hamilton, one of the greatest to ever race and a multiple-time world champion for Mercedes, was famous before, his popularity skyrocketed—at least within the confines of our apartment—after the series came out.

Allegra loved the Mercedes team principal, Toto Wolff, an Austrian with a thick accent and a penchant for doling out nuggets of wisdom in quick sound bites. His wife, Susie Wolff, was a former race car driver herself and also worked for F1. The show had scenes of them at home in the UK, living an ideal life as a racing industry power couple. Allegra had great affection for their collaborative marriage. She maintained an equal level of hatred for the Red Bull team and their cocky team principal, Christian Horner, and the team's star driver, Max Verstappen. Verstappen, a ruthless young upstart from the Netherlands with zero charisma, was threatening Hamilton's dominance. Allegra respected talent and ambition but not hubris. Scenes with Verstappen and Horner drew her disgust. Her interest started to transcend rooting for a favorite sports team and become something closer to rooting for the biblical triumph of good over evil. In those first few seasons of the show, which she fervently binged, good obliged. Things got dicier as time went by, as things tend to do.

The show began filming in 2019, each season airing several months after the racing season ended. Allegra watched them all in the latter half of 2021, while pregnant, then caught up to watch the races in real time every Sunday. That was a mistake, as Verstappen had begun winning. Not just sometimes but winning all the time, crushing the competition. Hamilton was an afterthought. She would watch the races and lament. She'd lie in bed with the blanket pulled up over her face and spout muffled hatred. Her beloved sport, taken over by a dullard.

I loved listening to Allegra talk about F1, somewhere between a gossip columnist and a sportscaster. I loved that, after everything, she was able to maintain that level of passion for anything, especially something frivolous. I was jealous. I always took everything so seriously.

I was looking forward to Brian visiting in October. He was DJing at a club in Brooklyn and would be flying in from Berlin. He tacked a few days onto the trip to stay with us in our new apartment. I think he wanted to check in. I needed it.

Allegra and I decided to drive to the airport to pick him up. When we got there, there was some confusion over which terminal he'd arrive at. The traffic cops were vicious, so we couldn't idle for too long. We kept driving in mindless circles around the airport as we waited for updates on Brian's precise location. We were listening to *Spiderr,* an album by Bladee. Pronounced "blade," Bladee is a Swedish musician whose real name is Benjamin Reichwald. He is ostensibly a rapper, but his music sounds like a teenager freestyling karaoke. Maybe that's why it sounded so good at the time, doing dystopian laps around JFK: Carefree is hard to fake.

Though I loved the reassurance of track two, "ITS OK TO NOT BE OK"—a ridiculous song whose only lyrics, repeated ad nauseum, were "Baby, maybe you can save me" and "It's okay to not be okay"—track six, "BLUE CRUSH ANGEL," upped the stakes. The lyrics were surprisingly touching:

I saw a rainbow in the dark
I put a symbol in a song
I put a window in the wall
To the statues in my mind,
Stand forever

"I put a window in the wall." The search for a way out. Was this song about me? The *Spiderr* album cover was an illustration of a shirtless guy with a Herculean set of abs and a luscious mane of hair, clutching a spider in its web. The spider has an enormous egg sac. The guy, you can sort of make out, has the Hebrew word for "truth" imprinted on his forehead. What did it all mean? Who knows, and who cares. Though I loved the music, the entire project of it felt so stupidly stoned, so wonkily post-post-postmodern as to be a joke. Or maybe this is how things go in blissful, problem-free Scandinavia? Nothing to worry about in a semisocialist Arctic utopia, so fire up the synthesizer and let's make some tunes.

I found out later that Bladee's life had not been as happy-go-lucky as I presumed. In 2015, he quit his job working at a kindergarten and moved to Miami, attempting to grow his music career alongside his friend and fellow Swedish rapper Yung Lean. In their early twenties and on their own far from home, the two started to heavily use drugs. One evening, Yung Lean fell into an apparent drug-induced psychosis. Bladee called for an ambulance. A few hours later, Barron Machat, Lean's twenty-seven-year-old manager, died in a car accident on the way to visit him in the hospital. Machat was found to have Xanax in his system. In the aftermath, Bladee moved back to Sweden and worked in a shampoo factory for a while. "I was not really OK," he told *The Guardian*.

A few years after Yung Lean's overdose (he survived) and Machat's death, Bladee found himself in Thailand, where he says, of all things, he was apparently struck by lightning. Or at least it hit very close to him. Either way, this close encounter with a lightning strike, that rarest of things, changed him. "I was sure I was gonna die, but I didn't, and it put me into this next level of seeing things in a weird way," he said in an interview. "I felt like an angel or something—everything made sense to me."

I put a window in the wall. I thought Bladee had stumbled onto this clarity, that his lyrics were nonsense poetry, that I had been the one to make sense of them. I thought that this Swedish musician was coasting through, noodling around, accidentally illuminating life's darker nooks. I was wrong. He, too, was in pain; he, too, was grieving. My belief, rooted in the depth of my own grief, was that, compared to me, everyone else had it easier. That might largely be true. But it doesn't matter. My own loss did not preclude others aching from wounds of their own. And some of those people were working hard to heal. *I put a symbol in a song.*

I played "BLUE CRUSH ANGEL" on repeat until we found Brian. Allegra had been texting with him as he deplaned, but it turned out she had missed the text where he gave us the final call on his new arrival gate. We'd been circling for nothing. Eventually we found him, and he was miffed after waiting, irritable after a long journey. I apologized, but Allegra laughed, didn't give an inch. It was so good to see him.

While Brian was in town, we'd wanted to see a museum retrospective of the German photographer Wolfgang Tillmans. I love Tillmans's photos. They're almost never of the same subject, but they're all sublime, lovely works of restlessness. He's photographed men and women naked in the woods, crawling up trees, free as fauns. He's photographed Chloë Sevigny, himself in a hospital bed, flowers. He has a series of photos of airplanes midflight as shot from the ground that I like even if I don't totally understand them. He has photographs that are not technically photographs but are swirls of color on photographic paper generated without a lens. They look like microscopic rainbows being born. The retrospective was titled "To Look Without Fear."

"My work is informed and sustained by acknowledging and enduring the extremely low probability of making a good picture," Tillmans once wrote in an artist's statement. This is either the demure hogwash of a genius or, for such a prolific maker of stuff, an acknowledgment of an inevitable truth: Most attempts at beauty are failures. Tillmans's career was evidence of a relentless push against the tide. If what he was saying was true, every successful photo on display was accompanied by a multitude of unseen duds. Their hidden existence heartened me.

In addition to his visual art, Tillmans is a musician. He came up in the German electronic music scene, and many of his photos are of the euphoric moments people have in and around dance clubs. That experience so informed him that he began producing his own idiosyncratic, techno-adjacent songs. I love them deeply. My favorite is a song called "Insanely Alive" that I listened to constantly in the months just before Renzo's death. It was winter during the pandemic. Still a cold and fearful time, but not the worst of it. Allegra had recovered from the difficulties of his birth, and I'd found a new job. Renzo was happy in daycare. Everything was looking up.

One day, we noticed Renzo had a small red mark on his face, below his left eye. We first thought it was a pimple, but over a week or two it grew in diameter and did not go away. Because the skin around the protrusion was thin and because kids often rub their eyes, he started to make himself bleed regularly. It didn't hurt him, but the little wound would take forever to scab over, as he couldn't leave it alone. We once had to strap him into his car seat in the living room so he wouldn't squirm while we tamped him down with gauze. He hated that so much. We did too. We saw a dermatologist, who said that if he were an adult, she'd just zap it with a laser right there in the office. As he was a baby and thus unable to sit still, he'd instead have to go under anesthesia to have it removed.

Before the surgery, Allegra and I were unbelievably stressed, though ultimately there was no need to be. Everything went fine. Renzo would have a little scar under his eye. That was the worst of it. Getting through this trial made me love him and love her so much more. We could survive anything, I believed at the time. I'd play Wolfgang Tillmans's record at home, I'd look at Renzo, I'd look at Allegra, and I'd start to sing: "You are insanely alive. / You light me up. / You light me up." He says the last line twice to make sure you get it. He's barely even singing, repeating the chorus in his lighthearted German drawl. I deepened my voice to mimic him, which I did poorly but with great delight. Eventually Allegra and I were both saying it around the house, an inside joke masquerading as a profession of love. Or vice versa.

Insanely alive. I assume Tillmans did not mean "insane" as in mentally unwell, but in its slangy meaning, à la "You are *very* alive," "You are *extremely* alive." What a lovely compliment it is. You are *brimming* with aliveness. Your aliveness lights me up. This is what I meant when I sang it to Renzo, what I meant when I sang it to Allegra, and what I believe she meant when she sang it to him and to me.

I couldn't listen to that song again after Renzo died, but one of the rooms at the museum show was a video installation of Tillmans with his music blasting as a soundtrack. Standing in the museum, "Insanely Alive" felt relevant again, now in a new way. I was alive, insanely. "You light me up." He was singing about Renzo.

In the exhibition, there was an enormous photograph of Frank Ocean, the portrait Tillmans had taken of him in the shower that was used for the cover of *Blonde*. You can't see his face in the photo; he's covering it with his hand. *Try to know me,* his pose seems to say. It's a dare; you never will. But I did know him and I felt like he knew me. Teens were lined up in front of the photograph, taking selfies with Frank like he was their friend. They understood. I took one, too.

Tillmans's show also featured a self-portrait I truly loved. In the photo, he's standing in what looks like an empty parking lot in front of some trees, a power line. His T-shirt reads, "Incoporo a revolta," with the translation below, in parentheses: "I embody revolt." It's not the most flattering photo. Tillmans is unshaven and his shirt is soaked in sweat. Why include it in the show? I wonder if what he wanted to say was *Here I am. Against the odds, I have made it.*

As you leave the exhibit, you're confronted by a sculpture of sorts, what looks like a very tall set of mirrored cabinets. You have to pass by it on your way back out to the escalator. After you've looked at Tillmans's world, you're forced to look at your own. There he was, and now here you are. In the gift shop, I bought a T-shirt commemorating that show. Tillmans's name was on the back, and on the front it said, simply, "To look without fear." I wore it all the time.

That was Brian's last day with us before he left to go

back home to Berlin. He said he missed America. Both of his parents had died before his own son was born. He loved his fiancée and he was close with her mother, but it wasn't the same. In Germany, people were closed off. It was making him closed off. He said people there didn't get his jokes. Not being able to be funny was painful. He told us a story about how, after a waiter at a restaurant doubted his understanding of Thai basil versus regular basil, they got into a heated argument. There was yelling involved. All the pressure built up had to go somewhere. Brian was such a wellspring of light that it felt tragic to see it at all dimmed.

Allegra and I tried to convince him to get a therapist. I looked up therapists in Berlin who spoke English, therapists who were American and dealt with expats, familiar with the difficulties of integration. Within his small family, he was the only American, outnumbered two to one. His son understood English but responded in German. Things would change, but it was hard. It would take time. That moment, here we were, Allegra and I, sitting at a table, hoping to repay our debt to him for his tending to us. We could not be his parents, but for that evening we would try to be good friends. To be of use, for once not to need. We'd make the trip to Germany ourselves the next summer, we knew, for his wedding. By then, we'd have a new baby. *See you then,* we promised. In no time at all.

Because of the pandemic, most museums were closed during Renzo's lifetime, but we did bring him to Dia Beacon once, when he was about sixteen months old. The museum is about two hours outside of New York City, and we drove up in the Volvo to meet our friends Pete and Jolene, along with their daughter, Zia. She was a few months older than Renzo.

Allegra and I had learned Jolene was pregnant while watching soccer at a German beer hall. Jolene wasn't drinking and Allegra and I had our suspicions, but we kept them to ourselves. We needed to only briefly—she told us before we left the bar. We had our own good news to share with them some weeks after. It was the summer of 2019, and as Allegra and Jolene approached motherhood together, they'd pose for photos with their growing stomachs.

Eighteen months later, there they were, Renzo and Zia, fully formed humans, strapped into their strollers on a very rainy day in Beacon. The museum, housed in a massive former box factory, had an exhibit by the musician Carl Craig in the sprawling basement space, an original piece of techno that you listened to while standing in the middle of the room, four speakers hanging from the ceiling. On the floor, a literal *X* marked the spot where you were to stand and listen, soaked in sound, totally alone, doing something that you usually did in a room packed with bodies. A metaphor for Covid? Maybe one for life. Hopefully not.

We moved on to the room with the enormous Richard Serra installation and let Renzo and Zia out of their strollers so they could roam untethered. Serra is a sculptor of massive steel works whose enormity is hard to describe in words. Instead consider numbers: The first of Serra's three "torqued ellipses" pieces on display at Dia Beacon measures around twelve feet by twenty-seven feet. It is a sculpture made of hulking sheets of steel, browned by the elements. Serra has long made work like this, strong and big, the kind of things that feel engineered to be imposing and macho. Serra, who died in 2024, himself looked imposing and macho, with a pugilistic face and spherical bald head. I don't dislike his work, but I find it difficult to connect with. There is nothing loving about it. It is about totality, control, ego. I see it and think about the flatbed truck that must have had to haul it. The crane that lifted it. All those hours of communal labor for one grandiose vision.

After Serra's death, a consideration of his work framed the torqued ellipses as cathedrals of sorts, memorials created by a downtown New York City man, inextricably tied to the twisted metals of September 11. That feels right, as their ability to still be standing, from now to infinity, feels like a monument to continuation, to eternity. In that sense of immortality, his sculptures are impressive. But still, impressive in a threatening way. I wondered if they might somehow fall and squash me. If that happened, the sculptures wouldn't feel anything.

Because he was a little boy, what Renzo saw was different. To him, the sculptures were not huge, sadistic hunks of metal but a playground. So he wanted to play. At the time, he was still wobbly on his feet but, recently motivated by the perambulation of his little peers at daycare, had started to rapidly steady. Zia, though a few months older, was spending her time home with her parents and had not quite as confident a strut. But she must have been inspired watching Renzo zoom in and out of Serra's ellipses, and she hopped to it.

The two of them happily waddled in and out of the

sculptures, up and down the length of the gallery. It was joyful to watch. An early bout of Stendhal syndrome.

When Renzo and Zia finally tired themselves out, we parked them on a bench and fed them snacks. One of the four parents took a photo—I don't remember who—and it froze that moment in time, Renzo in the quilted green jacket he preferred over all others. His hair was a dreamy mop. Zia, beside him, showing off the cartoonishly chipmunky cheeks she'd grow into soon enough. But for now, they looked like the children they were. They'd grow up friends, we hoped, able to prove the longevity of their relationship with a snapshot from the day they ran circles around Richard Serra. It was a nice day, the kind you imagine you'll have when you think about having kids.

Sometime later, after Renzo died, Zia's father, Pete, made a watercolor of Renzo based on that photo. Pete took up watercolor during the pandemic, and it turned out he's really quite talented. In the painting, Renzo is sitting up straight. He's wearing the green jacket and his white Nikes with the red swoosh. He's holding a stuffed avocado toy; the avocado is smiling. His hair, his famous hair. He looks so handsome. When I look at the painting now, I see my son, whom I love deeply and miss so much it hurts me everywhere, every day, even still.

I also see Pete's bold brushstrokes. I see the way he subtly has managed to have the green of Renzo's jacket emerge from the black background. I see the attention to detail in his depiction of Renzo's two little front teeth. I see my son, yes. But I also see something else, and that is a work of art.

Before the new baby, out of an abundance of caution, Allegra had done what is called a CVS test, a procedure where a doctor inserts a long, thin needle into a pregnant woman's belly and extracts cells from the placenta to be tested for genetic abnormalities. The test would also tell us if the baby was a boy or a girl, though it would not tell us if or when lightning would strike again.

The test was done on a Thursday morning, and the doctor said he would call by five on Friday evening if he had the result, and if not, he would call sometime Monday. As five approached, Allegra and I waited. Five came and nothing. We were frustrated to have to wait the weekend, another two days in the dark. Allegra wanted to stay in; I wanted to go out. This was not an especially high-stakes disagreement, but typically we would have compromised, one acquiescing for the sake of the other. We didn't do that that night. The pressure was too great. Somewhere out there was news of our future, undelivered to us. At that point, with lack of control the underlying theme of our lives, doing anything other than exactly what we each wanted was going to be impossible. So we didn't. Allegra stayed home and I went out.

I met up with my friend Katie for a beer. Katie was a new friend from work. She was young, inherently wise. She was curious about people and a big music fan, often out at clubs. I liked hearing what DJs she liked and didn't, living vicariously through her. Hanging out with her made me feel not so old, or so alien. It was nice to be in her company.

Katie and I ordered burgers. I was hungry. Then Allegra called me. It was six thirty. The doctor had called after hours because he knew we'd want to know. I was flooded with guilt for not being with her. But that's what happened.

"It's a girl," Allegra said. "She's okay." There were no abnormalities, nothing to fear.

I cried. Katie did, too. Aside from the doctor, Allegra, and me, she was the first person to know.

It was a relief that the baby would not be a boy. I feel ashamed to say this, as though I am betraying my son, but it meant, at least, she would not look exactly like him. The thought of that had been too much to bear.

Though I knew I soon would be, I did not yet feel ready to be a father again. I'd made some progress, but the void of grief was still too great. I still needed to be pampered, entertained, fed, and watered. *Bless this coming child,* I thought, but she was a stranger. I could imagine the far future, this baby at fifteen, twenty, thirty, forty, fifty, sixty years old. A graduate, a bride, a mother herself. I'd be dead, and she'd remember her father who always loved and supported her. We would get there; the inevitable would come to pass. But at the moment, my belief in the reality of a newborn was more slippery. Wonderful but unbelievable. Not part of the routine. Not yet.

Allegra and I discussed names. Cookie, I wanted to call her. Because I love cookies. Like when you ask a four-year-old what to name a dog. Cookie.

A friend suggested Cosima, and we liked that. A supple name. Not technically Italian, but Greek. Close enough. We decided, for a nickname, we could shorten Cosima to Coco, which I found to be sufficiently Cookie-like. Cosima, with Simone for a middle name. Simone sounded nice. Nina Simone, Simone Biles, Simone Leigh: good company. A less freighted middle name than Rollins. She could be Coco Schnipper if she was a goof or, one day, drop the Schnipper and be Cosima Simone if she needed a stage name. It would be her life, up to her.

In the months before the baby came, I read the book *Also a Poet* by Ada Calhoun, daughter of the art critic Peter Schjeldahl. Calhoun discovered that her father, in the 1970s, had attempted to write a biography of the poet Frank O'Hara. Schjeldahl had interviewed scores of O'Hara's friends and contemporaries before the project was abandoned after facing roadblocks from O'Hara's notoriously prickly sister, who controlled his estate. Calhoun, upon finding her father's interview tapes, attempted to finish the book. She sort of did. The end result is not necessarily a biography but a book about many things: poetry, painting, New York City in the fifties, misogyny, and parenthood. I found it mostly to be about that last thing. Specifically about the fact that Schjeldahl was often a bad father. Time and again, Calhoun shares anecdotes where he values his writing and love of art over her.

Unsurprisingly, Calhoun's upbringing fell largely to her mother. Yet this book, critical of him as it was, was clearly for and about her father. His writing, his success, and his insatiable hunger for art are a story she feels compelled to tell despite his fatherly failings. The former possible because of the latter.

Schjeldahl died of cancer shortly after *Also a Poet* was published. When he first received his diagnosis, he wrote an autobiographical essay, "The Art of Dying." Ostensibly, as the title suggests, it's about art and about dying, but it's really about writing. "Writing consumes writers. No end of ones better than I am have said as much," he wrote. "The passion hurts relationships. I think off and on about people I love, but I think about writing all the time." What a miserable thing to say. What an honest thing to say. It scared me, but it entranced me a little, too, the blurring of devotion and duty. It's not for nothing Calhoun herself became a writer.

Reading the book, I felt for her. I also took her experience as a warning sign. When Renzo was born, I was not worried about my fidelity to him. I had been waiting for him my whole life. A baby! My baby. I'd have happily traded any ounce of selfhood to ensure his happiness and well-being. But something had changed since his death. I hadn't asked for a period of time freed from the day-to-day constraints of parenting, but I'd gotten it. Reading *Also a Poet,* I recognized within me some of the singular obsession with art and writing that defined Schjeldahl growing in me. He would have gone to a hundred La Monte Young concerts in a row if he wanted to, fatherhood be damned. Was that who I was now? Before Renzo died, I would have said no, but now I was not so sure.

With most people, I felt needy, ungenerous, prickly. Brian understood, but he lived in Germany. Allegra understood, but she was grieving like me. The realm of the human was otherwise freighted with expectation and disappointment. I could not help clocking the attention I was or was not getting from family and friends, keeping score of how much I was on people's minds. It felt grubby and pointless yet unavoidable. To balance the emptiness of Renzo's death I'd instead tapped into the aesthetic world, which gave and gave and did not ask for anything in return. As I got used to relying on that, I worried that I'd have trouble giving it up with the arrival of a daughter. Whatever had caused Schjeldahl to be a cultural font, he did not give an inch in the face of parental responsibility. Self-care or selfishness? I'm willing to bet he never considered the question.

Frank O'Hara understood. "I am the least difficult of men," he wrote. "All I want is boundless love."

In 2019, a little more than a year before Renzo was born, I interviewed Henry Rollins about his own love of music. It was over the phone, for a piece about records that had influenced his life. We started when he was young and made our way across the years. He spoke eagerly about working to resolve his anger as he got older.

He said he started listening to calmer music, and it began to act, he said, like a "balm." Then he had a revelation. It was time to stop performing such aggressive music, to stop toting his rage around from stage to stage. "Around 2004, I woke up one morning and went, 'Wow, I'm done with music,'" he said. "Little by little, I went back to being a music fan. . . . I got happy about music again, because I was no longer making it. I'm way, way better off. Still not the happiest guy on the team, but not prone to bouts of anger like that. I get depressed because that's just how I'm wired. But it's not the Sturm und Drang and it's not the roller coaster. Maybe the testosterone level is starting to fade, as my hair can't get any whiter. I still hate men and want to fight them but, knowing that any sixteen-year-old could kick my ass, I have to remain peaceful."

It's imperfect progress, still tinged with the shadow of violence, but it is progress nonetheless. There is the old adage that time heals all wounds. I don't think that's true. What time does is to enable erasure. It forces you to forget, or perhaps enables you. Time may erode your anger over the cause of the wound, but it won't heal it. That you have to do yourself. I was ready to no longer hold on to my anger about Renzo's death, but how? And what would replace it? What I envied in Rollins was his decision to change. He realized he wanted to be a different person, and so he became one. It seems like it should be more complicated than that, but maybe it isn't.

I knew Rollins himself had battled grief from reading *Get in the Van* as a boy, though it had been decades since I'd read it. Before our daughter was born, I decided to revisit his story. I hoped I could learn something from how he made it through.

On a December evening in 1991, Rollins and his best friend and roommate, Joe Cole, were walking home from a visit to the corner store. It was meant to be a quick trip; Cole had popped some bread in the toaster before he left the house. As they headed back to their place in Venice Beach, they were met by two men with guns who demanded money. Cole and Rollins didn't have much on them, so the robbers sent Rollins inside the house to get more. Rollins has said at that moment he imagined that both he and Cole would be killed while the house was robbed. As he entered the house, from behind him, he heard gunshots. He took off, fleeing out the back door. Rollins, still unsure of Cole's fate, found a phone and called the police, who arrived soon after. Cole, who had been shot, died outside. Despite an exhaustive investigation, the men responsible for the murder were never found.

After Cole's death, Rollins published two books largely about grief, *See a Grown Man Cry,* an impressionistic collection of writing (some of which was composed before Cole's death), and *Now Watch Him Die,* which is mostly a diary. I slowly read them both. I found the loneliness, rage, and confusion in Rollins's writing to accurately reflect my own experience of loss. He was angry at all times, powerless to defuse the electricity of his emotions. I identified with his ire and exasperation, similarly to how I had looked up to him as a boy. But now he was closer to a peer. We were two grown men working out how to move forward after experiencing the sudden, up-close death of a loved one. Our losses were different, but the severity of them, the shock, were the same. I don't think it's presumptuous of me to say I know how he felt.

When he died, Cole was thirty, as was Rollins. The two men were very close. Cole joined both Black Flag and Rollins Band as a roadie on multiple tours, and he and Rollins lived in the house in Venice Beach together. Rollins has described Cole as having an approachable lightness, easily getting people to open up to him. When he died, Cole had been working on a project photographing and interviewing the homeless population of the neighborhood, many of them Vietnam vets. Not an actor or musician himself, Cole did not receive an obituary in any major publication. The things that make a life notable to the public I guess he had not yet been able to accomplish. But his murder was covered in the news. "Punk Rock Band's Road Crew Member Slain," read a headline in the *Los Angeles Times*.

> A Venice man who once served on the road crew for the defunct punk rock band Black Flag was shot to death Thursday by robbers as he walked home from a neighborhood grocery store, police said.

> Joe Cole, 30, and his roommate were returning from the Boys Market on Lincoln Boulevard at 12:40 a.m. when they were robbed of about $40 by two gunmen, said Lt. Ross Moen. The victims were then ordered to return to their house about 1½ blocks away, where one of the suspects fired a single shot at Cole and fled, Moen said.

Rollins is not named. The next paragraph, the third and final, mentions that Cole's father was a TV actor and calls Cole a "popular figure in the alternative music scene."

Not long after his murder, *Unsolved Mysteries* aired an episode about the case. "A late night trip to the corner store becomes a terrifying descent into an urban hell," the host says. Rollins appears in an interview, filmed close up. The top of his head is cut off, like they couldn't contain his entire being. He talks in his typical monotone, like he's desperately holding himself back from exploding in rage. "Within one second, you are going from your ninety-millionth trip to the grocery, home, to two guns in your face." This is a literal description of what happened, but it's also a good description of how sudden death feels.

As a grieving father, listening to Black Flag, to Rollins Band, I reconnected with the music's anger and disgust. It was a relief; I was not alone. Henry and me. He helped me articulate my feelings of disconnection from the rest of the nongrieving world and the oblivious privilege they lived. We were two citizens of the same fucked-up planet.

I can now name the feeling I related to, was so inspired by, in Henry Rollins's music as a boy: uncompromisingness.

When you are a child, even one not saddled with sickness, you lack agency. Rollins's music promised freedom. It offered me a portal. The alienation I felt from my middle-school peers was easy enough to reframe as self-reliance. It's easy to romanticize feeling alone as a teenager, when actually you live with your parents. As a grown man, grieving, that isolation had begun to feel dire. When death shows you how alone you actually are, there's little charm in it.

"I know I am not capable of telling anyone what I feel and what fury and anguish courses through my veins during every waking moment," Rollins writes in *Now Watch Him Die*. It feels like you can open the book up to any page and find a grotesque, bodily description of his grief. "Sometimes I feel like I am suffocating inside my skin, like I should be ripping out of it," he writes. "I hope my fury won't turn my bones to ash. Even if it does, it won't change a thing." It's worth noting that he does, at least, endorse forward momentum. "Keep walking the trail."

Rollins may have been an angry and depressed person before Cole's death. Fighting those demons is what made him such a captivating musician early on. But I think the immutability of grief after Cole's death powered his later career in a new way. I know the difference between the anger you get from depression and the anger you get from grief. The former is oblique; the latter is sharp and hot.

In August of 1994, Rollins Band played at the massive outdoor Reading Festival in the UK. Footage from the performance is on YouTube. Clips from the festival aired on TV, and before they played, a scruffy British man introduced the band from the studio. "We leave you tonight with the Rollins Band, rocking Reading '94 with 'Volume 4,'" he says. His chipper tone is almost comically incongruous with the music to come. "Until next week, sweet dreams!"

The performance is mesmerizing, but it's difficult to watch. "Volume 4" is a song about the disconnection Rollins felt between himself and his fellow man in the wake of Cole's death. It gives me pangs of recognition. It makes me feel bad for him. It makes me feel bad for me.

Rollins sings much of the song's final verse bent over at the waist, squeezing the microphone with both hands like he's wrestled down a venomous snake. The song contains no beauty. It's just about powering through. You have to seize the day before it seizes you.

> I used to be alive but I threw it all away
> I used to have problems, I used to live a lie . . .
> I used to have a mind, I used to wonder why
> But now I go from day to day and wait around to die
> like he did

One way to read this is through the lens of misery. But there's an element of escape, too. He used to have problems. But how can you have problems when nothing matters anymore? He watched his best friend die. I watched my son die. After that, what can even come close to mattering? Once you've lived through the worst life has to offer, you have nothing else to lose.

It feels upsetting to say, but that realization contains a hint of unburdening. You can take that one of two ways: nihilism or freedom. The former is likely self-explanatory; the lure of the abyss is difficult to resist. The latter, which gives grief a tinge of silver lining, has been one of the hardest things to comprehend; it's horrible to imagine that grief may come with a gift. But when you know nothing can ever hurt as badly, you don't have to live as tentatively. And if somehow it does, you know you can survive. You're living proof.

In *Now Watch Him Die,* Rollins explains how miserable but essential it felt to perform such deeply personal music, even if it was for an often-indifferent audience. His tone as a writer is often bitter, sometimes petty. He must have known how churlish the writing would come off—in a brief preface before the book's tour diary section, he says it was "written under the influence of Death, exhaustion, repetition, shame, guilt, paranoia, fear, alienation, rage." But also "the overwhelming will to survive and endure." I desperately wanted to know how all these ideas could coexist. I thought the book might provide a new insight. And it sort of did. "Play hard as fuck," he offers as a note on performing, though that kernel has greater utility than just as a musical insight.

Rollins is uncompromising. I admired his ability to stay both defeatist and optimistic and to use these conflicting emotions to keep making music, to keep writing, to be useful. He had an undeniable and inspiring need to create, perform, exist. But he did that while being wholly antagonistic to the general population. A difficult balancing act of love and hate, but an example of the perils of succumbing to nihilism instead of embracing freedom.

He has enemies. Police, the audience, people who work at clubs, people who work at record labels. Sometimes his own bandmates. He hated the people who killed Joe; he had dreams of shooting them. But they were long gone; he couldn't take it out on them. So the rest of the world would suffer instead. I saw the usefulness in having someone to hate. I'd seen how easily hate came if I indulged it. My patience for anyone's problems that didn't end up in the sudden death of a child wore thin. People I had once thought were a little self-involved I now saw as thoroughly frivolous and stupid. Idealists were privileged daydreamers. The war in Ukraine had begun some months after Renzo's death; my response to photos of families fleeing was to envy those who got to leave with their children. I felt shame for these feelings, but I still felt them. Whatever was soft inside me before had hardened. But Rollins wasn't soft to begin with. "Depression drives a car into my back," he writes in *See a Grown Man Cry*. "I take Death seriously / Not life." I both feared and hoped I'd end up like him. Was it better to be alone, miserable but productive, or to live a useless life among people who would never understand you? Truth or compromise?

But his life had little warmth. Throughout his books, he writes of moments where interacting with people pains him. A group of fans being kind to him after a concert is cause for consternation. He looks at a pile of fan letters and envies that the fans have someone to write to. Where was *his* Henry Rollins?

As I kept reading, what I had initially seen as inspirational, this jackhammering through to the other side, I began to see as a cautionary tale. Rollins's survival came with costs.

Derision can be fodder for art, but it doesn't make you a pleasant person. "I think that more people should get stabbed in the face with screwdrivers," he writes after a contentious conversation with a crowd member at a show in Holland. "Fuck all of you. I hope you all get raped and murdered, fucked in the ass and slaughtered."

This made me feel gross. I'd named my son after this guy? I wasn't sure what I'd been thinking. Why had I emailed him? What did I expect him to say? Why had I sent him a photo of Renzo? Did I think he and I were going to be simpatico as we tiptoed through the daisies, comparing grief stories? What did I expect from him? He was a real person, yes, but he was not my friend. I was a fan. He did not owe me anything. Neither did anyone else, I realized. I'd need to accept that to move forward. I'd also need to accept that I wanted to move forward.

All revelations are painful; you don't get to eat the apple without being cast from the garden. What I was learning was that no one knows better about you than you. Not even your heroes. Not even Henry Rollins. He didn't have any more answers than I did. In fact, his answers were probably worse. The reason I felt like shit all the time was because my son died suddenly. Not because I was going about fixing it wrong. Not because other people weren't helping me enough. I had a roof over my head, health insurance, friends and family who cared. I needed to remember that, appreciate it. While Rollins's descent into misery and isolation was tantalizing, it was a fantasy. I didn't want to be fueled by spite and disgust. I didn't want to be angry anymore. I'd always been a friendly guy. That wasn't good or bad; it was true. The sooner I accepted that, the sooner the grief could settle in for the long haul. Because no matter what I wanted to change about myself, Renzo's death would not change, not ever.

~

To be clear, Rollins remains my lifelong hero. Black Flag reunited without him. He said in an interview that "doing the music was like gladiator sport." When I interviewed him in 2019, he said that being a musician wasn't good for him, or for the world. "There's so many people I was rude to out of anger, insecurity, or feeling so depressed, I was just not making sense," he said.

It's a relief to hear. He changed. By extension, so could I. But how do you overcome the death of your child? When grief first arrives, it's all-consuming. Eventually, for better or worse, it isn't.

This is what I know now. Everyone has their own struggles, their own pain. They deal with it however they can. Everyone is doing their best. Give yourself grace; give it to others if you can. I said once after Renzo died that I no longer felt human. I may have wanted that to be true, but it wasn't. Grief did not disqualify me from my humanity; it confirmed it. I am just like you and you are just like me. If I can get through this, you can get through anything. I wish I didn't know that, but I do. Rise above.

They have names for everything. The Paleolithic Era. Permafrost. The guillotine. Antiperspirant. Wind. Romance. Sometimes the same thing can have multiple names. Are you going to watch a film or a movie? Do you feel cold or chilly? Innocuous enough. Sometimes people disagree about the words, so they change them to get you on their side. Climate change? Global warming. Pro-life? Anti-choice.

When you're sick, you search for a diagnosis, a name for what ails you. It puts the pain in a container. Do you have a migraine or a sinus headache? Crohn's or colitis? Stage III or stage IV? A name is an organizing principle. Third grader, fourth grader, fifth grader. New York Knick. Golden State Warrior.

In college I would say, "My roommate will be home later" or "Those beers are my roommate's." Then she said to me, "Please use my name." She was a person, not a concept. Jess.

Brother, sister. Mother, father. My father's mother, Grandma Bess, speaking of my mother's mother, Grandma Rita, noted that there is no word in English for the relationship between the parents of a bride and the parents of a groom. She said there is one in Yiddish: *machatunim.* To some people, this was a relationship important enough to name.

When your spouse dies, if you are a woman, you become a widow. If you are a man, you become a widower. I have to imagine the feeling is pretty bad, regardless of gender.

When Allegra and I started dating, she became my girlfriend and I became her boyfriend. Then we were fiancés, though we never used that word, and then spouses. Husband and wife. I do call her "my wife" sometimes, a put-on with good-natured affection. "How is my beautiful wife doing today?" She calls me babe. Babe, can you run downstairs? If I don't hear her from the other room, which is most of the time, she'll raise her voice and switch to calling me Matt, my own name like a light punishment.

Renzo Rollins Schnipper. When he was born, Allegra and I became parents. I became both *a* father and *his* father. When he died, were we still parents? Everyone insisted on it. But when your spouse dies, are you still married?

There is no name for the parent of a child who has died.

Why not? Is it so rare an occurrence that language has had no need to label it? That seems unlikely. There are surely more parents of dead children than there are billionaires, and I know what to call them. I hear about them all the time. If we had a name, would people talk about us?

One night a few weeks before our daughter's birth, walking toward home, Allegra told me she didn't want me to look at my phone in the hospital, as I had consistently done over the preceding months at appointments while we waited for her perpetually late OB. I didn't know what to say. I was embarrassed. We walked home in silence. I knew I looked at my phone a lot. Doesn't everybody? In the moments she was referencing, slumped in a folding chair, still in shock and terrified to be back in a medical facility, I'd shrunk myself down and dived, dolphin-like, into the screen. Was that not okay? My phone was a device for momentary obliteration. From the outside maybe it looked like I was doing the crossword or scrolling TikTok, but what I was doing was probably closer to doing drugs, hoping to huff something that would let me briefly disappear.

At that moment on the street, it felt like what she was asking me to do was to not survive. But what she was actually asking me to do was to support her. Simple enough. But had I not been doing that? And, if not, what did that look like?

The entire year had been spent figuring out how to live our lives as best as possible, given the circumstances. We operated in parallel as much as we did as a unit. Tenderness between us was paramount, and abundant. But our attention was about to have new demands. When the baby was born, I'd need to support my wife, who'd need to support our daughter. Who was going to support me? A selfish thought I couldn't bat away.

We tried to make some adjustments to ease the transition. We hired a night nanny, Patricia, to help us out and keep us company. When we interviewed her, on a video call, she was sitting on the stairs outside her apartment and she held the phone on her lap, pointed straight up her nose. There was something reassuring about her limited knowledge of technology. She worked exclusively with newborns. She loved babies. Her clients were spread across the U.S., some out of the country, and she was in high demand. She also happened to live nearby and had a hole in her schedule before a job in New Jersey and another in California. Patricia would work with us for a month, seven days a week, 7:00 P.M. to 7:00 A.M. To us, night still meant death. If we could avoid it, or at least have a guide to ease us back into the morning light, the chances of survival were higher. I mean this literally.

We were privileged to be able to afford Patricia. Of all our fears about our daughter's birth and the time after, most were uncontrollable. But the few things we could control, we did. Ahead of the birth, Allegra had taken care to buy new everything. Bottles, pillows, books, clothes. Our daughter's world would be her own. We would not reuse anything of Renzo's. We did not want to erase him, but we needed to choose when we'd visit with him, and anything he'd touched was a reminder. The exception was his diaper pail. We had one that was easy to use and didn't stink. When we took it back out, we found it had a speck of his poop on it. Allegra cried, and then she cleaned it off.

After the difficulty of Renzo's birth, we had wanted to make sure Allegra could get pregnant again at all and, if so, if it would be safe for her. She had found this new OB, the late one, recommended to her as the doctor the hospital called in case of an emergency. To me, he was almost irritatingly nonplussed. During her first appointment, she relayed the story of her difficult labor and delivery. She'd lost a lot of blood, she told him. He looked up her file. He was unimpressed. A tragedy to us, another day in the office to him. She'd torn her uterus, we told him, distressed. "That's how they get the baby out," he said.

As her due date approached, it was decided Allegra should have a scheduled C-section, to be on the safe side. "What if you get Covid on the day of the delivery?" Allegra asked the doctor. Not going to happen, he said. "But what if?" He refused the notion outright. Nothing would go wrong, he assured us, an annoying bit of overconfidence that proved out.

Allegra's C-section was textbook. Her only major complaint about the whole thing was that the doctor had played Don McLean's "American Pie" over the speakers during the procedure. The "This'll be the day that I die" refrain was not well received. I was in the operating room, sitting beside Allegra's head, just as I had been with Renzo. There was a big photo mural on the wall of the New York City skyline, which I realized I'd seen before. Coincidentally, Renzo's sister was being born in the same room he had been. I still don't know what to make of that.

We stayed with the name Cosima. Coco for short. We went home after three days in the hospital. Allegra was recovering nicely. No infection. Patricia joined us on our first night home. She had a great vibe. I'd greet her at our apartment door, and we'd ride the elevator together. "Good evening," she'd say, and then laugh. She'd arrive in her street clothes and change into scrubs. She had multiple pairs in different colors. Strawberry red, baby blue. "Doing good?" I'd ask her. "Yes, yes, dear," she'd say. She liked to repeat words. "Princess, Princess Coco" she called Coco. I don't think she meant she was a double princess, but it had a lovely ring to it, the echo. It reminded me of Princess Leia, who had a noble calling. All princesses do.

Around ten at night, Patricia would take Coco into her bedroom, bringing her back to Allegra to breastfeed every few hours throughout the evening. We were not first-time parents—Patricia knew this—but she treated us delicately, showed us patience, and gave us guidance as if we were. In the early evening, she showed us how to bathe Coco, with a setup beside the sink that included a cushion, a diaper pad, a towel, micellar water, cotton rounds, and an assortment of pastes and lotions. We'd just plopped Renzo into a big plastic bucket. I'd watch Patricia bathe Coco in the sink and offer help, which was politely refused. So I'd stand beside Patricia at the counter, and talk to her about her own family, her daughters and her two grandsons, and the seemingly endless brood of babies she'd cared for. Then she'd bring Coco back to her bedroom and rock her to sleep. Allegra would rest in between feedings, eat, shower. I ate dinner and slept. Once a week I'd watch the new episode of *The Last of Us,* an HBO show based on a video game about a virulent strain of fungus turning people into zombies that technically is also about what happens to a father after he loses a child to a sudden death.

The first anniversary of Renzo's death was on Christmas Eve, as every subsequent anniversary would be. It was miserable if uneventful. Allegra's parents were sick with Covid, and plans to be with them were canceled. Instead, a few friends came over. Coco, not even two weeks old, slept beside me in the living room. The time passed.

I kept a diary around that time, and I wrote this on Christmas:

> The anniversary of Renzo's death was yesterday. I had been waiting for it basically the whole year. I'm not sure what I expected. Some deeper level of sadness? Some kind of cosmic tunnel to open up where I could feel beside him? Instead, I just felt like the day was a marker of what it was: the day where I had now completed one of every single day in a year without him. I now look back at this day a year ago and see myself in the wake of his death. The only thing to look back to now is loss.
>
> Of course that's not entirely true. But I couldn't even look at his photo yesterday. Seeing him brings back the realization of how

> strikingly alive he was and yet I know clearly that he no longer is. I feel like if I have been falling off a cliff the last 365 days, maybe I hit the bottom. That does not mean that I want to climb up to the top. It just means I live down here now.
>
> I get sad about not feeling sad. Feeling sad means I am connected to him. Not feeling sad means time is passing. I wanted to say it feels like I am moving on, but it's not me. It's time, the world. I wish to be where I was, with him.

Reading this now, it hurts to realize I did not mention Coco. But she was still so new.

Patricia took Christmas off. It was scary to be on our own at night for the first time. A dangerous time. Not long after dark, Allegra started to feel sick. She was shaking, cold, and nauseous. The doctor had said she might experience shakes following Coco's birth, but it had been two weeks. We called his office. It didn't make sense, he said. We should go to the emergency room. That was a thought worse to Allegra than whatever was happening to her. I bundled her in blankets. Her teeth chattered, her lips went blue. Something wasn't right. Coco was crying. I tried to feed her from a bottle, her first time. It didn't take.

We called our friend Jenny, a physical therapist, a mother, and a calm authority. She came over quickly, held Coco, and managed to feed her. I felt useless, tried to tend to Allegra, who suddenly asked me for a bowl. A big one. I brought her the one we use for salad with guests. Then she sat up in bed and vomited. She immediately felt better. The chattering stopped, her color returned. Was it anxiety? Food poisoning? Grief? Unclear. But it was purged. Jenny went home. Patricia returned the next day, and we extended her time with us for two more weeks.

Eventually, we got our sea legs back by brute force. Diaper rash, tummy time, cradle cap. It all came back. Coco was a sweet child, often incredibly hungry. Aside from her gluttony, she was relatively chill, didn't cry much. Allegra recovered relatively quickly from her C-section. She'd bought Coco a cheery wardrobe of pastel onesies with hearts, stars, fruit. Mauve was her color, white too. All along, we waited for the other shoe to drop. It never did. That nothing was wrong, nor would be wrong, was hard to accept. In some ways, this was even harder to accept than Renzo's death. Catastrophe was an event you could point to. Its lack was not. Letting your guard down was an admission you had faith, and we were no longer so naïve as to believe. Still, we did our best. Days passed as they do for most new parents, exhaustingly, beautifully. The only difference for us was that most people who have their second child still have their first.

In the early mornings, I'd carry Coco to the living room window and describe what was happening outside. Our apartment overlooks a large intersection. We'd watch the sun rise and wait to greet our first pedestrian. *Good morning, woman in the yellow shirt! Hello, tall man with a shaggy dog. Coco, look at the runner going so fast! Coco, look at the boy on the bike!*

Then, one day, *Coco, look at the man in the red winter hat pushing a stroller. Coco, it's . . . Michael Cera! Michael Cera appears to have had a second child. Good for him. Coco, do you see Michael Cera, messenger of time's ceaseless march, out taking a walk? Coco, say "Hello, Michael Cera."*

I picked up her little hand and waved.

After two months, Coco was newly able to hold her head up. She'd also started to smile. I'd been waiting for this moment, for the time when I'd look at her and she would look back at me, and we would truly see each other. I liked to lie on my back on the bed and hold her with my arms outstretched, our bodies parallel. She was still small enough that my hands could wrap around her middle, like I was cradling a big sandwich. As I held her aloft, I'd tell her stories about Princess Coco, intergalactic warrior for peace. In her baby Superman pose, she'd fly from the left side of the bed—*zoom*—to the right side—*zoom*—as she left Earth to fly to faraway planets mired in turmoil. The first place she'd fix was Costanzania, a world ruled over by the evil despot George Costanza. Because of his self-consciousness about his baldness, he forced all of his citizens to shave their heads. No one would possess enviable locks. Everyone was smooth-headed and miserable. But what about toupees? Could that help the dictator regain his confidence? Upon touching down, Coco discovered toupees had not yet been invented on this planet. She could fix this. Coco has a great head of hair, so she plucked out a strand and used it as a magic seedling to create a lush toupee, which she gave to Costanza himself. He looked great! With newfound confidence, he came to his senses about his oppressive ways and allowed everyone to grow out their own hair and be themselves. He thanked Coco for healing his soul, as well as his planet. A job well done, she flew back to Earth because it was time for a nap.

We got permission from Coco's pediatrician to give her solid food early, at four months old, because the way she eyed our plates went beyond lustful to something closer to full-on psychotic. The gap between desire and satiation can be a long one to traverse; when you finally get to your destination, the real thing can have trouble measuring up to your imagination. Not to Coco, for whom every crumb was a feast, literal kernels of knowledge swallowed by the fistful. God, she was a cute little meatball. Every part of her body was round and squishy. Sometimes she looked like a big-cheeked doll. I loved her with an intensity so difficult to wrangle that, at times, it was nearly impossible to look at her.

I could accomplish unthinking tasks: change her diaper, read her a story, push her in the stroller. But in the pockets of time when life slowed and I would see her, say, hold her hands in front of her face and consider them, I found it to be debilitatingly overwhelming. Her existence, after the death of her brother, was a miracle, a miracle in the way the universe is a miracle, unknowable and entirely out of my control. Looking at her was like staring at the sun. I would hold her tiny hand and quickly go from feeling happiness to feeling like I was going to implode, like my soul was being squeezed in a vise. The size of the loss of Renzo was the size of my love for Coco, but they did not cancel each other out.

One day, walking down the hall, I picked Coco up and held her over my shoulder. Renzo used to love it when I did that. Allegra took our photo. Coco looked like me. Two round-faced goobers. I posted the photo on Instagram. "That baby stole your face," a friend replied. I was curious what she would do with it.

~

I got tickets to see a concert with my friend Jason, the photographer who had rescued me after my post-therapy meltdown. We share a love of a guy who goes by the name Wicca Phase Springs Eternal, a musician from Scranton, Pennsylvania, otherwise known as Adam McIlwee. He'd been the droll singer of a rock band before starting Wicca Phase, a solo project where the music he makes might nominally be categorized as rap. More so, it sounds like the random spew of an intense, sensitive guy performing with minimal skill but great conviction. I identified with him.

I'd been nervous to go out to the concert for the evening and leave Allegra alone with Coco for the first time, but she knew how much I loved Wicca Phase and encouraged me to go. So I met Jason, along with his wife, Meghan, at the venue, which was an unventilated and blisteringly hot photo studio. We were by far the oldest people there.

There were several opening acts before Wicca Phase, and

we waited, sweating, for him to perform. The stage was barely elevated, so we stood on chairs toward the back of the room to see over the crowd. When Wicca Phase came out, he was wearing a leather jacket, a commitment to cool over comfort. He was onstage alone, pacing. His music had taken a turn lately, away from the eccentric and toward something with a sheen. I think he wanted to be taken more seriously. I appreciated that desire but not necessarily the aesthetic decision-making that accompanied it. Listening to him croon, I longed for his sloppier songs, imperfect but heartfelt. "I am in pain and I keep it a secret" was one of his early lyrics. I loved its plain confession. I also understood that no one wants to feel that way forever.

When Wicca Phase was on his second or third song, I noticed some commotion in the crowd, a security guard escorting a seemingly inebriated concertgoer to the exit. A moment later, I saw him collapse. He tried to get back up, failed, and fell again. Someone started screaming to stop the music. Meghan, a nurse, ran to the fallen man. "Does anyone have any NARCAN?" she yelled into the crowd, referring to the nasal spray that can reverse opioid overdoses. A punk-looking woman ran to her and pulled some out of her backpack. Meghan administered it and began to give the guy CPR as security guards cleared the room. Jason and I left and waited on the sidewalk across the street. In the distance, we heard sirens.

I started to panic. A whiff of death. I cried. But there was nothing to do but wait. After ten minutes, Meghan came out. The guy had responded to the NARCAN, though it took two doses. He was headed to the hospital to get checked out, but she imagined he'd be fine. I never found out if that ended up being the case. It was not my emergency.

In the spring, we began to plan for Brian's summer wedding in Berlin. We'd been looking forward, cautiously, to the trip since before Coco was born. By leaving his family and traveling to New York to be with us after Renzo died, Brian had helped us realize a path forward was possible; it was crucial that we go to Germany to celebrate him as he walked a new path himself. He'd never met Renzo, and we had yet to meet his son, Miles. It couldn't continue like that. The trip was a pilgrimage.

It was also an international flight with a six-month-old, which presented all sorts of opportunities for worry. With Renzo, we had never really traveled anywhere, due to the pandemic. A couple of trips in the car to and from Cape Cod. He knew what a plane was. He pointed to them in the sky. But he never flew. The idea that we could just stick Coco on a flight was exciting and terrifying, a microcosm of the experience of being her parent.

Allegra had a multistep plan to minimize the potential stressors of flying with a baby. A blackout tent for the bassinet, a shoulder bag to pack up the stroller. She'd feed Coco upon takeoff and landing to reduce any discomfort from the change in air pressure. We'd arrive at the airport early and stalk the check-in desk as the bulkhead seat, with the bassinet, was first come, first served. We bought Coco a few new toys to be unveiled on the airplane itself, something fresh to obsess over. We got her a cloth tissue box with little handkerchiefs to pull out, a simulation of her favorite activity at home. I appreciated Allegra's diligence about the trip but hunkered down for what I imagined would be an inevitably brutal eight hours across the ocean. Alas, after months of anxiety and preparation, the morning before we were supposed to leave, I tested positive for Covid. My first time. We'd have to miss the wedding.

Brian had asked me to give a speech. At my own wedding, five years earlier, Brian had given one, largely focused on our first year in New York as roommates. He did not, as I had expected, discuss the foundation of our friendship, based on the difficulties we both found in our lives as we transitioned to adulthood. Instead, he spoke at length about our building's super, a man named Shorty, who had once shown up at our front door trying to sell us a giant trash bag of pornography.

I wasn't feeling as lighthearted about my speech. I wrote it a few days before we were set to leave and was crestfallen that I would not be able to deliver it in person. So I asked a friend to give it on my behalf, and she obliged. There's video proof of this, but I have yet to gather the strength to watch it. But rereading it, I feel a combination of pride in both of us, with a tinge of embarrassment for the level of brazen earnestness. But only a tinge.

> We in America have missed Brian since he moved permanently to Europe, but seeing him, even afar, grow his family has been a blessing. As I've become a parent and a spouse, I have

> relied upon him for comfort, perspective, love. When my family suffered an unimaginable loss, Brian got on a plane and came to be with us. His then-girlfriend and now-wife Gigi supported him in that time, knew that she had to let him be there for us. It's what makes a partnership work. It helped my own partnership with my wife stay healthy. We will never, ever forget that time you all sacrificed for us, lending us your husband and father. But as we get older there is more heaviness, more emotion. It doesn't mean there is less joy, but that it is often much harder-earned.

We knew we still had to go to Berlin, to make the journey, and so we rescheduled for late August. By then, Coco was eight months old, almost nine. She was crawling feverishly, desperate to walk unaided. She'd hoist herself up on chair legs and toddle briefly with great gusto. She fell constantly but was uncowed. She seemed to almost revel in these failed attempts, as every face-plant meant she had given it a go. We were worried she'd be squirmy on the plane, but we'd miscalculated the reasoning behind her fanatical push for mobility. It was not purely physical but mental, too. She wanted the autonomy to explore. So she loved the plane because it was an entirely new and fascinating world of people, lights, screens. She wasn't upset at all. She wanted to hang out in the back galley, waving at everyone who came to use the bathroom. The flight attendants loved her. One asked to hold her, which we'd not normally let a stranger do, but, we figured, where could she go on a plane? She took Coco for half an hour. They took selfies and snuggled. When the flight attendant returned Coco, she was covered in her makeup. She gave Coco a Delta Air Lines pin, which she loved playing with, but we had to take it away to make sure she didn't accidentally stab herself.

We had no agenda in the city. See Brian and Gigi, meet Miles. Berlin was a backdrop. We ended up taking Coco to the newly reopened Neue Nationalgalerie. In the basement was a show of Gerhard Richter paintings, one hundred of his blurry, smudged works. I thought of how Renzo would have been able to identify all the colors Richter had used: red, yellow, blue. Coco was not yet talking. In another gallery was the work of Tehching Hsieh, an artist who, among other things, once spent a year punching a time card every hour of every day. At each punch-in, he took a self-portrait. The gallery walls were covered with them. He missed a handful of punch-ins, as he was asleep, but most hours were accounted for. In the photos, his hair got progressively longer, but that was about all that changed. A lot had changed for us in a year, but that doesn't mean the same is true for everyone. Eventually, after a series of grueling performance pieces, Hsieh gave up art and opened a café.

We all went out for pizza, two families of three. It was a warm evening. Berlin is a pale city, but this restaurant was at the top of a hill beside an orange bridge. The sky was blue in the way you always hope for. The pizza was good. After dinner, we strolled back down the hill in the dusk. As he walked, Miles held Coco's hand in the stroller, a blessed international meeting of the minds. Brian and Gigi put us on the bus back to our hotel, a short drive down the road. Then, two minutes later, the bus stopped violently short. The driver was trying to avoid a car suddenly backing out of a parking space and into traffic. He didn't quite hit it, but he might as well have. A majority of the passengers, Allegra and I included, went flying down the aisle. Allegra scraped her knee and elbows and I jammed my finger, which later turned a series of ugly colors. Nothing that bad. But we had not seen what happened to Coco. We rose to find she was in her stroller, thankfully still upright, and screaming.

"Does anyone speak English?" Allegra yelled to the dazed bus riders. The woman sitting beside Coco responded in German. "Do you speak English?" She was in shock. But she switched to English. The woman said she had fallen across Coco's stroller. The worst that happened was that her purse had possibly grazed her. Coco started to temper herself. She seemed okay. The bus driver walked down the aisle, said some things in German we didn't understand. The driver of the car came to the front door of the bus and the bus driver barked at and then dismissed him. Everyone sat down and the bus kept going. We stayed on. It was only two more stops to the hotel.

Back in our room, Allegra called Coco's pediatrician. It was still daytime in America. She said we should go to the emergency room. When the bus stopped short, Coco could have been jostled, and something could have happened to her brain. It was unlikely, but it was possible. Though she appeared fine, appearances could be deceiving, she told us, and it was better to be safe than sorry.

There was a hospital a block away from the hotel. As we

walked in, we saw several people from the bus, including the woman who had fallen over Coco. Thekla, she said her name was. She was cradling her elbow gingerly. She'd had a hard day, she said, even before the bus incident, and had been on her way to the symphony when the accident happened. "You should still go," I told her. The music would help. She couldn't fathom it. I felt like she was making a mistake. But she could make her own decisions. She said she was concerned about Coco. This emergency room, it turned out, didn't see children. We'd have to go to another part of town. I wrote down her email address and promised to write to let her know Coco was okay, as I presumed she was. I could process no other outcome, a positive outlook I clocked as something like progress. I called Brian, who soon met us in a taxi with a car seat, and we headed out.

My main memory of the second emergency room was the heat. I know Europeans are not big on air-conditioning, but this was another level of hot. Big, thick, disgusting air. We were there for hours marinating in it. It was way past Coco's bedtime and she was sweaty and cranky. She was crying, but we were not especially concerned. We knew she was just tired.

Brian and I took her outside for some air. She kept crying as we strolled her around the hospital grounds, but she seemed okay. She had to be. It didn't make any sense that she would have gotten a brain injury in a bus accident in Germany. That just was not going to be how our life went.

After a few hours, when she was finally seen, the young emergency room doctor confirmed there was no sign of injury, internal or external. She said we were to monitor Coco for unusual behavior over the next twenty-four hours, especially vomiting, though she imagined that was unlikely. And it was. Coco was fine. No brain scan necessary, no treatment at all. No lightning strike. We had caught a break. I did not take it for granted. I emailed Thekla to let her know Coco was fine.

But I was worried about Allegra. Had the accident crushed her spirit enough that we would no longer be able to enjoy our trip? Should we call it a day and return to the safety of home? No, it turned out. Her fervid determination, lately used to sniff out danger, was now going to be used in service of pleasure. We'd come all the way to stupid Germany, and we were going to have fun.

After Renzo's death, my love for Allegra had commingled with my grief. I no longer felt love untinged by despair. But at that moment, in Germany, I was amazed by her. She would have run through a wall to make sure we had a good time. I would have run through a wall for her. I loved her then as I had before, in the pure, unencumbered way I had when we first met and fell in love. Before children, before any of this. She was a determined woman. I loved that about her. It made me want to keep being a part of her life. Of life in general.

The next morning, we got up and took the subway to meet Brian at a Turkish market on the canal. It was chaotic, overflowing with vendors and shoppers, but Allegra wove Coco's stroller through the crowd like it was nothing. Because it was nothing. There's a photo of Coco, Brian, and me that Allegra took that afternoon. She hates being in photos, but she takes really nice ones. The three of us are sitting on a bench outside the market. I'm holding Coco. We're all staring into the camera, smiling. I remember feeling so incredibly happy at that moment. In the photo, I'm wearing my Wolfgang Tillmans shirt.

When we returned home to New York, I quit my job at Vice. The company had declared bankruptcy. I was spending most days filling out court-mandated spreadsheets logging money owed to freelance writers. It took weeks to color-code in order of priority. Desperate writers sent emails pleading for their money. It felt terrible to tell them we had no idea when or if they would be paid. Once I got to the end of the backlog, I'd had enough. I figured I could stay and go down with the ship, get laid off, and get severance and unemployment, but I wanted autonomy over what happened next. It was time to do something else.

Allegra started planning Coco's first birthday party early. The theme would be Formula 1. Formula *1,* for her first birthday. She found a bakery that would make a cake with pink fondant, racing flags, and silver stars. They sent over schematics for approval. Gluten free, but Allegra swore their cakes were so rich you'd never know. We also ordered a celiac's nightmare's worth of pizza, along with cases of seltzer in flavor combinations heretofore unimagined by reasonable people. Months ahead of the party, banners arrived in the mail, stacks of bamboo plates and silverware. We're a shoes-off household, so Allegra fashioned two-tiered shoe racks out of cardboard boxes and masking tape. Balloons were considered but abandoned. They would be lost on Coco, we decided. Upon reflection, that seems a ridiculous litmus test to have used. It's not like she would know what was going on otherwise.

There was the guest list to consider. Both sets of grandparents, Allegra's brother and his wife, my sister and her newly adopted daughter, my grandmother, who would likely not make the trip from Connecticut. Our neighbors, with their blond-haired, blue-eyed angel daughter, Cleo, six months older than Coco, who loved to hug Coco and whisper her name. Best Friend Rachel and her boyfriend, Joe. Molly, who, daily, after Renzo died, would send me photos of her aging dog, Ava. Molly had driven us to the hospital for Coco's delivery, and Ava died the day after Coco was born. Molly had to be at the party. (She ended up being out of town.)

Who else did we want to be there? We couldn't invite everyone. Could we? Discussing this with Allegra became a strange catalyst to taking stock of our relationships. We'd made new friends, shed old ones. Were people absent from our lives, or were we absent from theirs? Had things changed, or had we?

As Coco's birthday approached, I began to dread the party. What I had imagined would be a celebration now felt like a demarcation between our past and present selves. Renzo's parents, now Coco's. The same people, but not really. That metamorphosis was not necessarily something I wanted to have to consider with a roomful of people. Who is a child's first birthday party for, anyway? Certainly not the child.

In a way, I think Coco's party was for Renzo. Allegra wanted Coco to have a birthday party because Renzo didn't get to have one. Simple as that. His first birthday, in February of 2021, was in the middle of the pandemic. No guests. We did get him a cake, but nothing crazy. Carrot cake. We figured we'd have time for something sweeter. We were wrong to be optimistic. Was that optimism's fault or our own? Having a child at all was the human embodiment of optimism. No one could call us pessimists now. "You make plans and god laughs." Right in your face, it turns out.

Coco, at least, was turning out to have a good sense of humor. She'd been a good-natured infant, but we assumed that was infancy, not her. As she morphed into a toddler, though, lightness appeared to be a true part of her personality. She was clever and curious. Shoes were interesting, cords were interesting, hangers, the laundry basket, the off-limits territory of Mommy and Daddy's bathroom. What unknown treasures could it possibly hide? She stood at the doorway while we brushed our teeth and gazed in awe. Her eyes, wide open, with those long eyelashes, with her little mouth agape to display two bottom teeth (the others were late in showing up, the only thing she's ever done behind schedule). She gazed with great passion at every stuffed animal, at every dog on the street, at other babies in strollers, and at bananas (the absolute love of her life). At the playground, in the swings, she'd point to other parents, urging them to push her. Allegra and I had to gently ask on her behalf. "She's very friendly." She had a lust for life I was frankly jealous of. She contained not need but desire.

She was a loud child who made frequent use of her vocal

cords, long, sustained babbles coming from her mouth as she toddled around the house. She would gather her stuffed animals in her arms, two dogs and a bunny, her brood, going back and forth between her bedroom and the living room. Sometimes she'd use her shoulder to drag heavy bags, like a huge sack of building blocks or Allegra's backpack, weighted down with her work laptop. Coco looked like she was doing some sort of weight-lifting exercise she learned at a baby gym. She delighted in ripping up magazines, releasing high-pitched and satisfied shrieks at the sound of paper shredding. She was ticklish in her elbows and thighs, laughed with great satisfaction when we would swoop in on her from above.

"Gentle" is a word whose meaning we spent some time trying to instill in her. Gentle with your books, gentle with the dogs in the park, with the next-door neighbors' cats. "Gentle, sweetie," I can hear Allegra saying to her. We never had to explain that to Renzo. He was always gentle. They were different people. Of course they were. Sometimes, though, she looked exactly like him, especially from the bridge of her nose up. That wasn't a bad thing, though it made me confuse loving her and missing him. But we were determined to let her lead her own life. It was a complicated situation, literally impossible to explain to her. There was plenty of time to get there. For now, we tried to enjoy our time with her. She did not make that hard, at least. "She has presence," my grandmother said, with an air of takes-one-to-know-one recognition. "Vivacious," Allegra called her.

"You get the child you need," one friend said about her. She meant that the magic touch of this baby, with her inborn ridiculousness and enviably smooshy face, was the gift Allegra and I deserved. I appreciated that observation, carried it with me for some time. Then one day, all of a sudden, I wondered what it said about Renzo.

Coco loved her birthday party. Cake and a roomful of people doting on her. I'd been wrong to think the party would not be for her, that she'd not comprehend its occasion. Maybe she didn't yet grasp the "birthday" part of a birthday party, but the "party" part of it, absolutely. Allegra had dressed her in a lavender jumper with a white daisy print. My father fed her forkfuls of cake. She looked like a big girl as she ran from person to person, a two-foot-tall hostess. I was filled with love and pride, misery and grief.

The party ended at 2:00 P.M. sharp, when it was time for Coco's second nap of the day. Guests filed out of our apartment. The house was suddenly empty, and we were alone with Coco on her first birthday, as we'd been with Renzo on his. One trip around the sun. Her first. Hopefully of many. There was no reason to imagine that would not be the case. We took her out of her jumper and put her into her sleep sack and down into her crib. Her bedroom is in the back of our apartment, away from the street, and it was silent, like the party had never happened. Exhausted, she fell right asleep.

Two weeks later would be the second anniversary of Renzo's death, also a Sunday. By then he'd have been gone longer than he was here. Coco didn't know that, of course.

We talked to her about him all the time. How he could sit still when she couldn't. How they both loved the same blue chair and waving at buses. How I worked so hard to get both of them to laugh. To be happy. How I desperately missed him but, oh, how I loved her.

She didn't understand a word we said. She was untethered from language, comprehension. It was a freedom I envied. She had plenty of time left as a baby, plenty of time before she was old enough to understand the concept of a sibling, let alone the concept of death. It would be several years before Allegra and I sat her down and explained to her what would surely change her life, as it had changed ours. We would live in anticipation of that day, the clock ticking away. Further from his life, further into hers. How far is a light-year? We would find out.

There's one more song I want to tell you about. It's by the band Sonic Youth and it's about Joe Cole. Henry Rollins was not the only musician to write a song in his memory.

Formed in the early 1980s, Sonic Youth were avant-garde stalwarts and onetime Black Flag labelmates whose members had gotten to know Cole on tour. Their music was usually made up of hurricanes of guitar squall, but on some songs they pushed through the fog of feedback to coagulate into something sweet and sublime. As a teenager in love with the violence of hardcore punk, I found their music to be a worthy sibling, an answer to what sits on the other side of rage.

The band released two songs about Cole on their album *Dirty,* one each sung by guitarist Thurston Moore and bassist Kim Gordon, who were then husband and wife. "100%" opens *Dirty.* It's Moore's song. It begins with a cringey admiration for Cole's powers of seduction. "I can never forget you / The way you rock the girls." A fine enough song, but not the one for me. I much preferred Gordon's tribute, which is buried at the end of *Dirty,* track thirteen of fifteen. "JC," Cole's initials. It's as if she couldn't bear to say his name.

Gordon sing-speaks the song's lyrics. She sounds clipped, pained. "Arms around each other's back / You know that I liked you Jack." It's a lament. "A second here and then you're gone / Quicksand, quicksand all around." It was a song for Joe Cole, yes, but for all loved ones. In a 1992 live performance of the song, Gordon introduced the song as malleable in its dedication. "This next song is called 'JC,'" she said. "For John Coltrane, Joe Cocker, Johnny Carson, Julia Cafritz, and Joe Cole." Carson didn't die until 2004, Cocker until 2014, and Cafritz, a musician friend of Gordon's, is still alive. Love is a slippery thing. Not everything has to make sense to be true.

I came to think of "JC" as being about Renzo. "That wasn't how it's supposed to be," Gordon sings. Who else could she be talking about but him? "A sun-kissed boy that gave no thought." That part couldn't literally be about Renzo, actually. We kept him out of the sun fairly diligently. He had a blue bucket hat with a chin strap he wore to the beach. Still, I loved imagining him as sun-kissed in spirit.

Gordon wrote a memoir in 2015, *Girl in a Band,* and in it she touched briefly on her friendship with Cole and on writing "JC." "When Henry called to tell me about Joe, I burst into tears. I didn't get over it for a couple of years, to be honest," she writes. "The senseless, random act of violence against someone full of life and innocence was mind-blowing, and I hated Los Angeles for a long time after that." Gordon was from LA. She had been devoted to the city; it made her who she was. Grief could make you hate anything. About the song, she writes only—needs only—one simple and devastating line: "It was hard to sing without tearing up." But she did it.

The end of "JC" has a line that, more than anything I have ever heard, sums up the destruction of grief, the beauty of life, every big thought about purpose and lack thereof I've had since Renzo died, coiled up and shot through like an arrow. "You're walking through my heart once more, don't forget to close the door," Gordon sings. The guitar comes in, a sour elegy that takes its time to fade out. Don't forget to close the door, Renzo. But please know that I will always leave it unlocked.

Acknowledgments

Thank you to my wife Allegra Farina, to my parents, Michael Schnipper and Ida Schnipper, to my sister, Sara Schnipper, and to my grandmother Rita Mitrani. Thank you to Anthony Farina, Marianne Farina, Nicholas Farina, and Kimberly Farina.

Thank you to my editor, Marie Pantojan, as well as to Ben Greenberg, Azraf Khan, and Andy Ward at Random House. Thank you to my agent, Soumeya Roberts. Thank you to Michael Agger for editing the essay that led to this book and to Simon Greenberg for bringing it to Random House's attention.

Thank you to Daniel Arnold for the cover photo and Cassie Vu for the cover design. Thank you to Bill Callahan for reading the audio.

Thank you to early readers Jessica Arcangel, Sam Hockley-Smith, Hua Hsu, Katie Way, Amy Weiss-Meyer, and Anna Wiener. All of your insights made this a better book.

Thank you to the baristas at Prima and at the Center for Fiction, the two places where I wrote most of this book.

Thank you to my friends Raphaela Beeton, Dean Bein, Amber Bravo, Molly Butterfoss, Liza Corsillo, Jenny Donahue, Kevin Donahue, Katie Drummond, Hal Ebbott, Gigi Fakunmoju, Alex Frank, Jayson Greene, Stacy Greene, Alexandra Gurvitch, Rachel Hahn, Jolene Kao, Andrew Kuo, Jacob Long, Kate Lowenstein, Peter Macia, Cameron Mesirow, Leo Miller, Matt Murray, Lindsay Nash, Jason Nocito, Amanda Petrusich, Amy Phillips, Brian Piñeyro, Brian Shimkovitz, Michael Tutek, Bela Zecker, Naomi Zeichner, Michael Zelenko, and Cat Zhang.

Thank you to Henry Rollins.

About the Author

Matthew Schnipper is a New York City–based writer, editor, and Depop dealer. He writes the newsletter *Deep Voices*.

About the Type

This book was set in Sabon, a typeface designed by the well-known German typographer Jan Tschichold (1902–74). Sabon's design is based upon the original letter forms of sixteenth-century French type designer Claude Garamond and was created specifically to be used for three sources: foundry type for hand composition, Linotype, and Monotype. Tschichold named his typeface for the famous Frankfurt typefounder Jacques Sabon (c. 1520–80).